W9-AZR-073

POCKET GUIDE
TO APA STYLE

FIFTH EDITION

Robert Perrin
INDIANA STATE UNIVERSITY

CENGAGE
Learning

Australia • Brazil • Mexico • Singapore •
United Kingdom • United States

CENGAGE
Learning·

Pocket Guide to APA Style,
Fifth Edition
Robert Perrin

Product Director:
  Monica Eckman

Product Manager:
  Kate Derrick

Content Developer:
  Karen Mauk

Content Coordinator:
  Danielle Warchol

Product Assistant:
  Marjorie Cross

Media Developer:
  Cara Douglass-Graff

Brand Manager:
  Lydia Lestar

Market Development
  Manager: Erin Parkins

Content Project Manager:
  Rosemary Winfield

Production Manager:
  Samanatha Ross Miller

Art Director: Marissa Falco

Manufacturing Planner:
  Betsy Donaghey

Rights Acquisition
  Specialist: Ann Hoffman

Production Service:
  S4Carlisle, Mahendran
  Mani

Text Designer: Dare Porter

Cover Designer: Dare Porter

Cover Image: SuperStock/
  Masterfile

Compositor: S4Carlisle

For product information and
technology assistance, contact us at
**Cengage Learning Customer & Sales
Support, 1-800-354-9706.**

For permission to use material from this
text or product,
submit all requests online at
www.cengage.com/permissions.
Further permissions questions
can be emailed to
permissionrequest@cengage.com.

Library of Congress Control Number: 2013949231

ISBN-13: 978-1-285-42591-7
ISBN-10: 1-285-42591-X

Cengage Learning
200 First Stamford Place, 4th floor
Stamford, CT 06902
USA

Cengage Learning is a leading provider of
customized learning solutions with office
locations around the globe, including Singapore,
the United Kingdom, Australia, Mexico,
Brazil, and Japan. Locate your local office at
international.cengage.com/region.

Cengage Learning products are represented in
Canada by Nelson Education, Ltd.

For your course and learning solutions, visit
www.cengage.com.
Purchase any of our products at your local
college store or at our preferred online store
www.cengagebrain.com.

Instructors: Please visit **login.cengage.com** and
log in to access instructor-specific resources.

Printed in the United States of America
1 2 3 4 5 6 7 17 16 15 14 13

Contents

Preface

Pocket Guide to APA Style, 5th edition, is designed for students who need to write, document, and present papers in American Psychological Association style. This convenient and easy-to-use guide draws on the principles described in the corrected sixth edition of the *Publication Manual of the American Psychological Association* (2009). What sets *Pocket Guide to APA Style* apart from the lengthy *Publication Manual* is its overriding goal: This text presents the principles in a brief yet complete and easy-to-use manner. The guide is ideal for undergraduates who are working with APA style for the first time. Yet graduate students and working professionals will also appreciate its user-friendliness. To enhance its use, *Pocket Guide to APA Style* incorporates these helpful features.

- **Writing Scholarly Papers: An Overview** The introductory chapter of *Pocket Guide* describes basic researching and writing methods, serving as a brief review.

- **Manuscript Preparation** In one coherent chapter, *Pocket Guide* describes and illustrates all elements of an APA manuscript.

- **Editorial Style** In one convenient chapter, *Pocket Guide* explains APA guidelines for punctuation and mechanics (periods, quotation marks, capitalization, number style, and so on), general writing style (transitions, verb tense, and so on), and word choice (jargon, biased language, and so on).

- **Separate Documentation Chapters** For easy use, *Pocket Guide* provides separate chapters to explain reference-list entries for periodicals, books, audiovisual sources, and electronic sources.

- **Reference-List Entries and In-Text Citations** Chapters 4 through 8 include guidelines for documenting 59 kinds of sources, with 117 sample reference-list entries. These updated samples are followed by corresponding in-text citations.

- **Sample Papers** Two complete sample papers are included in *Pocket Guide,* one argumentative and one experimental; both include annotations related to manuscript form and issues of writing.

- **A Discussion of Plagiarism** With its student focus, *Pocket Guide* includes a discussion of plagiarism and ways to avoid it.

- **Appendices** Included in *Pocket Guide* are two appendices: one that describes effective ways to prepare PowerPoint and poster presentations and one that covers the essential technical issues writers encounter across the disciplines.

Acknowledgments

My work on the fifth edition of *Pocket Guide* was pleasant and productive because of the supportive, knowledgeable assistance of Content Developer Karen Mauk at Cengage Learning. I also thank Mahendran Mani, Project Manager at S4Carlisle Publishing Services, for his careful handling of the production work.

I am also indebted to the following people for their thoughtful reviews of the fourth edition of *Pocket Guide to APA*.

Joyce Adams, Brigham Young University

Marie Balaban, Eastern Oregon University

Pamela Brown, University of Central Missouri

Gerald Browning, Baker College

Kananur Chandras, Fort Valley State University

Debi Cheek, Rasmussen College

Brian Cronk, Missouri Western State University

Lori Davidson, Chestnut Hill College

Deborah Dessaso, University of the District of Columbia

Evaline Echols, Lee University

Daniel Fasko, Bowling Green State University

Robert Folden, Texas A&M University, Commerce

John Garot, Globe University

Kim Gunter, Appalachian State University

Cathy Hammond, Gordon State College

Martin Hyatt, ASA College

Thomas Kelley, Averett University

Brenda Kilpatrick, Alverno College

Charlotte Larkin, Texas A&M University, Commerce

Teresa Maas, Keiser University

John Marlin, The College of Saint Elizabeth

Jackie McGrath, College of DuPage

Vanessa Miller, Texas Christian University

Kathryn Myers, Saint Mary-of-the-Woods College

Sharon Perry-Nause, Tiffin University

Michael Rutledge, Keiser University

Kristen Snoddy, Indiana University Kokomo

Mary Williams, Gordon State College

Finally, I wish to thank Judy, Jenny, Chris, and Kate for their encouragement.

R. P.

The research process is a complex combination of thinking, searching, reading, evaluating, writing, and revising. It is, in many ways, a highly personal process because writers approach research activities by drawing on different skills and past experiences. Yet researchers often follow a series of connected phases (which nonetheless occur in a different order for different people).

This chapter reviews, in a brief way, the common steps that most researchers go through. If you are an experienced researcher, you can use this chapter as a "refresher." If your research experiences are limited, consider each discussion carefully as you proceed with your work.

1a   Subject and Topic

Research begins with a subject. In some academic contexts, you may choose the subject yourself, usually with the instructor's approval. But in other contexts, you may be required to choose a topic from a small number of suggested topics or be assigned a topic with a predetermined focus.

Guidelines for Assessing General Subjects

As you select potential subjects for your research (broad categories such as test anxiety, Internet crime, the effects of divorce, and so on), keep in mind these practical and important principles.

- **Interest.** When possible, select a subject that interests you. Do not spend time researching a subject that does not make you curious.

- **Length.** Select a subject that can be adequately treated within the length requirements of the assignment. You may have to expand or reduce the scope of your subject to match these length constraints.

- **Materials.** Select a subject for which you can find materials of the kind identified in the assignment. Be aware that you can use libraries other than your own for your research and that the Internet provides access to a broad range of materials, both traditional and nontraditional.

- **Challenge.** Select a subject that challenges you but that does not require technical or other specialized knowledge you may not have time to acquire.

- **Uniqueness.** Select a subject that is not overused. Overly familiar subjects stimulate little interest, and materials are soon depleted.

- **Perspective.** Select a subject you can approach in a fresh, interesting way. Readers will appreciate your efforts to examine subjects from new perspectives.

Narrow Topic

In most instances, you will need to narrow your large subject (test anxiety, for example) to a specific topic (test anxiety among middle school students) so that you can research selectively and address the issue in a focused way.

To discover ways to narrow a broad subject to a specific topic, skim general reference materials, paying particular attention to recurrent themes, details, and ideas. Then consider establishing a focus using selected strategies for limiting topics.

- **Time.** Restrict the subject to a specific, manageable time span—for example, school violence in the 1990s.

- **Place.** Restrict the subject to a specific location—for example, health care in rural areas of the United States.

- **Special circumstance.** Restrict the subject to a specific context or circumstance—for example, achievement testing for college admissions.

- **Specific population.** Restrict the subject to address its effects on a selected group of people—for example, depression among elderly people.

1b   Thesis Statements, Hypotheses, or Stated Objectives

To clarify the central goal of your writing, present your ideas in one of three alternative ways.

Thesis Statement

A thesis statement, sometimes called a problem statement, is a declarative statement (usually one but sometimes two or more sentences) that clarifies your specific topic, presents your opinion of (not merely facts about) the topic, and incorporates qualifications or limitations necessary to understand your views.

> Although the effects of birth order are always evident to some degree, other variables also affect personality, intelligence, and socialization.

Hypothesis

A hypothesis is a conjectural statement that guides an argument or investigation; it can be explored (and potentially proved or disproved) by examining data related to your topic. Conditional in nature, a hypothesis is assessed using available information.

> Students who delay work on major research projects until the last week are more likely to plagiarize than are students who begin their work early.

Stated Objective

A stated objective is a brief, well-focused statement that describes a research paper that presents information. Unsubtle and not arguable, it must define the topic clearly and narrow the topic when necessary.

> I will share a brief history of airport security in the United States, from the 1940s to the present day.

1c   Research Goals

Although most research is prompted by specific academic or job-related requirements, you should also think broadly about the goals for your work, recognizing that research provides multifaceted learning experiences.

Course-Related Goals

Course-related goals are broad in scope and establish the foundation of your research work.

- **Using the library.** Library research should take advantage of a full range of sources, as well as the electronic means to locate them (see pages 5–9).
- **Using the Internet for academic purposes.** Research requires that you learn to use the Internet selectively for scholarly purposes, which involves learning to evaluate the credibility and value of online materials (see pages 9–12).

- **Assessing source materials.** In a global way, research depends on evaluating materials critically to ensure that you use sources that credibly support your ideas (see pages 10–13).

- **Taking notes.** Research requires you to record ideas and information from your sources carefully and completely so that you can use them appropriately in your writing (see pages 13–20).

- **Responding effectively to opposing views.** Fair-minded research acknowledges and uses opposing views to maintain a balanced perspective.

- **Synthesizing ideas.** Effective research blends information and ideas from a variety of sources, thereby creating a comprehensive presentation that is better or fairer or clearer than the presentation in individual sources.

- **Incorporating material into writing.** Effective research leads to writing that incorporates ideas and information with clarity, accuracy, and style (see pages 21–24 and section 4f).

- **Citing sources accurately.** Research requires you to give proper credit to the people whose ideas and information you have used; this technically focused process requires attention to detail (see Chapters 4–8).

Professional Goals

Professional goals develop from the process of establishing a working knowledge in your field of study. As such, they focus on the acquisition of knowledge and specific skills.

- **Learning to use specific sources.** Research in each discipline requires familiarity with the kinds of sources that are respected and commonly used.

- **Demonstrating discipline-specific knowledge.** Research in each discipline builds upon accepted information that you must be able to incorporate fluently.

- **Using specialized formats.** Each discipline's research incorporates unique formats that you must learn to follow.

- **Using specialized writing styles.** Research in each discipline depends on specific stylistic patterns for presenting ideas and information.

Personal Goals

Personal goals concentrate on degrees of knowledge, improvement, sophistication, and experience. Although they are less easily quantified than goals matched to courses, they are also important.

- **Learning about a subject.** Exploring a subject through research improves your knowledge of your discipline.
- **Improving skills.** Conducting research gives you the opportunity not only to use your early research work but also to develop more sophisticated skills.
- **Expanding experiences.** Research work allows for varied kinds of personal growth.

Id   Research Methods

Methods of research vary depending on the project, but most projects require multidimensional work with a variety of sources. To complete such projects, take advantage of a full range of strategies.

The Library

Learn to use all features of your library, especially familiarizing yourself with the research areas that you will most commonly use.

- **Reference.** General source materials—dictionaries, fact books, encyclopedias, indexes, guides, bibliographies, and so on—that can guide your preliminary research. (Most reference materials are now available in electronic form.)
- **Catalog (computer).** Computer clusters where you can secure the records of library materials. (Almost all computer catalogs can be accessed from other locations.)
- **Stacks.** Bookcases where print materials (bound periodicals, books, and so on) are stored according to a classification system.
- **Current periodicals.** Recent copies of journals, magazines, and newspapers. (Most periodicals are now available in electronic form.)
- **Government documents.** Printed materials from national, state, and local government departments and agencies—books, monographs, pamphlets, reports, and so on. (Most government documents are available in electronic form through government websites.)

- **Microforms.** Microfilm and microfiche materials. (Many of these materials have been converted to digital forms.)
- **Media.** Audiovisual sources—DVDs, Blu-rays, CDs, and so on.
- **New books.** The area where new books are displayed before being placed in the general collection.
- **Special collections.** The area where rare books, archival materials, and other special sources are located.
- **Special libraries.** Discipline-specific collections that are housed in sublibraries.

Periodical Databases and Online Catalogs

Periodical databases (online indexes) allow you to gather technical information about—and frequently view full texts of—articles in journals, magazines, and newspapers. Online catalogs (electronic search systems) allow you to gather technical information about books, monographs, government documents, and other materials in the library's collection. Both periodical databases and online catalogs provide access to descriptive material about sources through keyword search techniques.

Keyword searching uses easily recognizable words and phrases (often in combination) to access sources. Computer systems search for keywords in titles, tables of contents, and other descriptive materials and then display "matches." To locate a broad range of materials, use alternative phrases (*collaborative learning, collaboration, team research,* and so on) as you conduct searches. Also explore Library of Congress listings, available online at most libraries, to discover unique category descriptions. For example, the Library of Congress system does not use the fairly conventional expression *medical ethics;* rather, its category notation is *medicine—moral and ethical aspects.*

Information About Periodicals

Most libraries now subscribe to a variety of periodical databases. These databases vary in design and format, but all provide a wide range of information about articles in journals, magazines, and newspapers. Most databases provide information about the following elements.

- **Article title.** Full title and subtitle of the article (listed first because some articles have no attributed authors).
- **Author.** Full name of the author (or authors).
- **Affiliation.** Professional affiliation (university, institution, and so on) of the author (or authors).

- **Periodical title.** Title of the journal, magazine, or newspaper.
- **Volume and issue number.** Volume (which indicates the number of years that a periodical has been published) and issue number (which refers to the specific issue in which the article appeared) for journals and magazines, but not for newspapers.
- **Number of pages.** Total number of pages of the article (in the original print format); alternatively, the starting page of the article.
- **Date.** Month/year, month/day/year, or season/year of publication.
- **ISSN number.** The 8-digit International Standard Serial Number (ISSN) of the article.
- **Abstract.** A short but detailed overview of the article, emphasizing key ideas and briefly explaining procedures.
- **Language.** The language in which the article is written (English, Japanese, Farsi, and so on).
- **Document type.** A brief description of the article (feature article, journal article, review, and so on).
- **Classification.** The article's subclassification within the discipline (child psychology, educational psychology, cognitive psychology, and so on).
- **Subjects or keywords.** Subjects or specific phrases in the article (medical ethics, juvenile delinquency, test anxiety, and so on).
- **Publisher or source.** A description of the periodical (periodical, peer-reviewed journal, and so on).
- **DOI.** The digital object identifier (DOI) assigned to the article.
- **Formats for articles.** Formats available for selected articles: HTML, PDF, summary, abstract (see page 8).
- **Database.** The name of the database that provides the digital record.
- **Options.** Choices for using the database record for the source (Save, Print, E-mail, and so on).

In addition to these common elements, individual databases provide other detailed information: the author's e-mail address, the database access number, the country of publication, the database identification number, the document URL, the number of references, the word count, the research techniques (tests and measures, age of research subjects, methodology), the publication history (date submitted, revised, and accepted), and the copyright.

You may never need all of the information provided in a database listing, but reviewing the full range of material will allow you to evaluate a source before retrieving it.

Format Options (Within a Periodical Database)

- **HTML.** Hypertext markup language. A digitized version of the article available on a website.
- **PDF.** Portable document format. A page-by-page scanned image of the article as it appeared in the printed periodical, available as a single file.

Information About Books and Other Library-Based Materials

Online catalogs provide standardized information about each source in the library's collection.

- **Author.** Full name of the author (or authors).
- **Title.** Full title of the source, including subtitles.
- **Facts of publication.** City, publisher, and copyright date.
- **ISBN.** The 10-digit International Standard Book Number (ISBN) if the source is a book.
- **Technical description.** Specific features—edition, number of pages, use of illustrations, book size, and so on.
- **Format.** Description of the source (book, book with CD, book with audiotape, and so on).
- **Subject classification.** Library of Congress classification, both primary and secondary.
- **Notes.** Descriptions of special features (bibliography, index, appendices, and so on).
- **Location.** Location of the source in the library's collection (general collection, special collection, or specialty library).
- **Call number.** Classification number assigned to the source (indicating where the source is located in the collection).
- **Number of items.** Number of items (three volumes, one volume with CD-ROM, and so on).
- **Status.** Information on whether the source is checked out, on reserve, on loan, and so on.

- **Options.** Choices for using the online catalog record for the source (Save, Print, E-mail, Add to List, and so on).

Many online catalogs provide links to websites like *Google Books*, which provide other kinds of information: reviews from readers, sources for buying books (Amazon.com, Barnesandnoble.com, and so on), a list of other books that refer to the source, other available editions, the table of contents, the length, the cost, and so on.

The Internet

Internet research may lead you to a scholarly project (a university-based, scholarly site that provides a wide range of materials such as full-text books, research data, and visual materials), an information database (a site that offers statistical information from governmental agencies, research institutions, or nonprofit corporations), or a website (a site designed to share information or ideas, forward a political agenda, promote a product, or advocate a position). (See pages 11–12.)

To navigate an Internet site successfully and to gather crucial information for a reference-list entry, learn about the key elements of an Internet home page.

- **Electronic address (URL).** Uniform resource locator—the combination of elements that locates the source (for example, http://www.aagpgpa.org is the URL for the website of the American Association for Geriatric Psychology).
- **Official title.** Title and subtitle of the site.
- **Author, host, editor, or webmaster.** Person (or people) responsible for developing and maintaining the site, if identified.
- **Affiliation or sponsorship.** Person, group, organization, or agency that develops and maintains the material on the site.
- **Location.** Place (city, school, organization, agency, and so on) from which the site originates.
- **Posting date or update.** Date on which the site was first posted or most recently updated (revised).
- **"About This Site."** Description of how the site was developed, a rationale for it, or information about those involved with the site.
- **Site directory.** Electronic table of contents for the site.

1e   Evaluating Sources

Because not all sources are equally useful, you should analyze them and select the ones best suited to your research. This ongoing process requires continued assessments and reassessments.

Print Sources (and Their Electronic Counterparts)

Print sources—journals, magazines, newspapers, books, and so on—have traditionally been the mainstay of most research; today, many of these sources are also available in electronic formats. Whether available in print or available in an alternative electronic format, these sources are the easiest to evaluate because of their familiarity.

- **Author's credentials.** Determine whether an author's academic degrees, scholarly training, affiliations, and other published work establish his or her authority.
- **Appropriate focus.** Determine whether the source addresses the topic in a way that matches your emphasis. Consider literature reviews to establish scholarly context and empirical studies to incorporate recent primary research.
- **Respected periodicals.** Generally, use journals with strong organizational affiliations; furthermore, note that peer-reviewed journals (those that publish works only after they have been recommended by a panel of expert reviewers) offer more credibility than non-peer-reviewed journals. Choose specialized, rather than general-interest, magazines. Choose major newspapers for topics of international or national importance, but choose regional or local newspapers for issues of regional or local importance.
- **Sufficient coverage.** Determine whether the source sufficiently covers the topic by examining its table of contents, reviewing the index, and skimming a portion of the text.
- **Reputable publishers.** University, academic, or trade presses publish most of the books you will use, which generally ensures their credibility. Note also that publishers often specialize in books related to particular subjects.
- **Publication date.** For many topics, sources more than 5 or 10 years old have limited value. However, consider establishing historical context by using older sources.

- **Useful supplementary materials.** Look for in-text illustrations, tables, charts, graphs, diagrams, bibliographies, case studies, or collections of additional readings.

- **Appropriate writing style.** Skim a potential source to see how it is developed (with facts, examples, description, or narration); also consider whether the author's style is varied, clear, informative, and persuasive.

Internet Sources

Although Internet sources provide a fascinating array of materials, some of the material posted on the Internet has not been subjected to scholarly review and is, therefore, not necessarily credible. As a result, you should use only Internet sources that meet important evaluative criteria.

- **Author, editor, host, or webmaster's credentials.** A website may or may not have an identified author, editor, host, or webmaster. If it does, however, explore the site for information about his or her qualifications to discuss the topic.

- **Appropriate focus.** Skim the website to see whether its focus is suitable for your topic. Sometimes the site's title makes the focus clear; at other times, an entire site has a general focus, but its internal links allow you to locate material on narrower aspects of the larger subject.

- **Sufficient coverage.** Review documents on the website to see whether the coverage is thorough enough for your purposes.

- **Domains.** Examine the website's electronic address (URL) to see how the site is registered with the Internet Corporation for Assigned Names and Numbers (ICANN). The following common "top-level domains" provide useful clues about a site's focus and function.

    .com – A commercial site. The primary function of a commercial site is to make money.

    .edu – A site affiliated with an educational institution. These sites may be posted by the school or by an individual affiliated with the institution.

    .gov – A government site. These sites present trustworthy information (statistics, facts, reports), but the interpretive materials may be less useful.

.mil – A military site. The technical information on these sites is consistently useful, but interpretive material tends to justify a single, pro-military position.

.museum – A site for a museum. Because museums can be either nonprofit or for-profit institutions, consider the purpose that the particular museum serves.

.org – An organizational site. Because organizations seek to advance political, social, financial, educational, and other specific agendas, review these materials with care.

- **Possible biases.** Do not automatically discount or overvalue what you find on any particular kind of website. Rather, consider the biases that influence how the information on a site is presented and interpreted.

- **Affiliation or sponsorship.** Examine the website to see whether it has an affiliation or a sponsorship beyond what is suggested by the site's domain.

- **Posting or revision date.** Identify the date of original posting or the date on which information was updated. Because currency is one of the benefits of Internet sources, look for websites that provide recent information.

- **Documentation.** Review Internet materials to see how thoroughly authors have documented their information. If facts, statistics, and other technical information are not documented appropriately, the information may be questionable.

- **Links to or from other sites.** Consider the "referral quality" that Internet links provide.

- **Appropriate writing style.** Skim the website to see how it is written. All sources do not, of course, have to be written in the same style, but it is an issue worth considering when you evaluate a source.

Audiovisual Sources

Because of the range of audiovisual sources available, use specific criteria to assess each kind of source individually. Many of the techniques employed for evaluating these sources correspond to those used for print and Internet sources.

- **Lectures and speeches.** Use criteria similar to those for print sources: speaker, relationship to your topic, coverage, sponsoring group or organization, and date.

- **Works of art, photographs, cartoons, and recordings.** Because these sources are used primarily to create interest in

most research papers, consider how well the image or performance illuminates your topic.

- **Maps, graphs, tables, and charts.** Evaluate these visual sources
the same way as you would evaluate traditional print sources.

- **Motion pictures, television shows, and radio programs.**
When these sources serve informative purposes, evaluate them
as you would assess print sources; when they are used crea-
tively, evaluate them using the same criteria you would apply to
other creative audiovisual forms.

Combinations of Sources

Although you must first evaluate your sources individually—
whether they are print, Internet, or audiovisual—your goal is to
gather a set of high-quality sources that together provide a balanced treatment of your topic. Consider these issues.

- **Alternative perspectives.** Taken collectively, the work of
your authors should provide a range of perspectives—academic
and popular, liberal and conservative, theoretical and practical,
current and traditional.

- **Varied publication, release, or distribution dates.** Include
sources that represent the information, ideas, and interpretations
of different periods, when appropriate.

- **Different approaches to the topic.** Combine sources that
range from the technical (including facts and statistics) to the
interpretive (providing commentary and assessments). Also
consider literature reviews for secondary analyses and empirical
studies for primary research.

- **Diversity of sources.** Incorporate a wide range of sources—
periodicals, books, electronic sources, and audiovisual sources—
to ensure that you have taken advantage of the strengths of each
kind of source. Be aware, however, that in some instances your
research must focus on selected kinds of sources.

Evaluating sources is an inexact process. No matter how carefully you review materials, some may later prove unhelpful. Yet
early efforts to evaluate sources generally enhance the focus and
efficiency of later, more comprehensive work, such as reading,
taking notes, and, finally, writing the paper.

1f   Note-Taking

Note-taking is an individualized process: different researchers pre-
fer different methods for recording information and ideas from

sources. However, all note-taking should be meticulous and consistent, both to avoid plagiarism and to simplify the subsequent writing of the paper. Consider alternative methods for note-taking and remember that note-taking must be complete, consistent, matched to the kind of material being used, and honest.

Before taking notes from a source, create a complete and accurate entry for the reference list. See Chapters 4–8 for guidelines and samples.

Methods of Note-Taking

Begin your note-taking by analyzing each note-taking system and choosing the one best suited to your specific project, library facilities, work habits, and instructor's expectations.

- **Note cards.** Note cards are easy to handle and to rearrange during planning stages, but they hold only limited amounts of information.
- **Paper.** Paper is easy to handle and has sufficient room for copious notes, but notes on paper are difficult to organize during planning stages.
- **Computers.** Notes on computers do not have to be retyped during the writing process and can be printed multiple times, but on-site note-taking with computers is sometimes awkward.
- **Photocopies and printed texts.** Photocopied and printed materials do not have to be recopied, and you can write on them. However, photocopying and printing can be expensive.

Complete Information

Record complete identifying information with each separate note to avoid having to return to a source at a later, and potentially less convenient, time.

- **Author's name.** Record the author's last name (and first initial, if necessary for clarity); for multiauthor sources, record only as many names as are necessary for clarity.
- **Title.** Record only important words from titles but use italics or quotation marks as appropriate.
- **Category notation.** Provide a brief descriptive term to indicate the idea or subtopic that the information supports.
- **Page numbers.** Record the page number(s) from which you gathered information. If material comes from several pages, indicate where the page break occurs. (A double slash [//] is

a useful way to indicate a page break.) Also indicate when an electronic source does not include pages.

Consistent Format

Record notes in a consistent format to avoid confusion at later stages of research and writing.

- **Placement of information.** Establish a consistent pattern for placing information so that nothing is omitted accidentally.
- **Abbreviations.** Use abbreviations selectively to save time and space; however, use only standard abbreviations to avoid possible confusion later.
- **Notations.** Note anything unique about the source (for example, no page numbers in a pamphlet or an especially good chart).

Kinds of Notes

Four common kinds of notes serve most research purposes. Choose among these kinds of note-taking patterns depending on the sources you use and the kinds of materials they include.

- **Facts.** A fact note records technical information—names, dates, percentages—in minimal form. Record words, phrases, and information in a simple outline or list format and double-check the information for accuracy.
- **Summaries.** A summary note presents the substance of a passage in condensed form. After reading original material carefully, write a summary without looking at the original; this will ensure that the phrasing is yours, not the author's. Double-check the summary note to make sure that your wording is distinct from the original.
- **Paraphrases.** A paraphrase note restates ideas from a passage in your own words, using approximately the same number of words. Write a paraphrase without looking at the original and then double-check the note to ensure that the phrasing is yours.
- **Quotations.** A quotation note reproduces a writer's words exactly. Double-check the quotation note against the original; the copy must be an *exact* transcription of the original wording, capitalization, punctuation, and other elements.

Sample Note Card

- Author's name
- Category notation
- Paraphrased information
- A quoted phrase
- Pages

Rohde   Family Stress

- Family circumstances (fighting, negative activities, unreasonable demands) can make adolescent depression worse.

- Family members must join in efforts to treat adolescent depression.

- "At times the therapist who works with the adolescent must maintain an alliance both with the teenager and the parents in the face of conflict between the two."

                                      p. 24

Rohde, P. (2011). Cognitive behavior therapy treatment for adolescents. In D. W. Springer, A. Rubin, & C. G. Beevers (Eds.), *Treatment of depression in adolescents and adults* (pp. 21–27). In *Clinician's Guide to Evidence-based Practice Series*. Hoboken, NJ: Wiley.

1g   Plagiarism

Plagiarism, from the Latin word for kidnapping, is the use of someone else's words, ideas, or line of thought without acknowledgment. In its most extreme form, plagiarism involves submitting someone else's completed work as your own. A less extreme but equally unacceptable form involves copying and pasting entire segments of another writer's work into your own writing. A third form of plagiarism involves carelessly or inadvertently blending elements (words, phrases, ideas) of a writer's work into your own.

- **Whole-paper plagiarism.** This kind of plagiarism is easily discovered. Through experiences with students in class, instructors learn what students are interested in and how they express themselves (sentence patterns, diction, and technical fluency).

- **Copy-and-paste plagiarism.** This kind of plagiarism is also easy to detect because of abrupt shifts in sentence sophistication, diction, or technical fluency.

- **Careless plagiarism.** This form of plagiarism is evident when distinct material is unquoted or when specialized information (dates, percentages, and other facts) is not acknowledged. Even when this is carelessly or inadvertently done, the writer is still at fault for dishonest work, and the paper is still unacceptable.

In all of its forms, plagiarism is academically dishonest and unacceptable, and the penalties for its practice range from failing individual papers or projects to failing courses to being dismissed from college to having degrees revoked. The seriousness of plagiarism cannot be ignored, so you must make a conscious effort to avoid this practice. To avoid plagiarizing, learn to recognize the distinctive content and expression in source materials and take accurate, carefully punctuated, and documented notes.

Common Knowledge

Some kinds of information—facts and interpretations—are known by many people and are consequently described as common knowledge. That Alzheimer's disease is the leading cause of dementia in elderly people is widely known, as is the more interpretive information that Alzheimer's disease is best treated by a combination of drug and psychiatric therapies. But common knowledge extends beyond these very general types of information to include more specific information within a field of study. In medical studies, for example, it is widely known that Prozac is the trade name for fluoxetine hydrochloride; in education, a commonly acknowledged interpretation is that high scores on standardized tests do not uniformly predict academic success. Documenting these facts, beliefs, and interpretations in a paper would be unnecessary because they are commonly known in their areas of study, even though you might have discovered them for the first time.

When you are researching an unfamiliar subject, distinguishing common knowledge that does not require documentation from special knowledge that does require documentation is sometimes difficult. The following guidelines may help.

What constitutes common knowledge

- **Historical facts** (names, dates, and general interpretations) that appear in many general reference books. For example, Sigmund Freud's most influential work, *The Interpretation of Dreams*, was published in 1899.

- **General observations and opinions** that are shared by many people. For example, it is a general observation that children learn by actively doing rather than passively listening, and it is a commonly held opinion that reading, writing, and arithmetic are the basic skills that elementary school students should acquire.

- **Unacknowledged information** that appears in multiple sources. For example, it is common knowledge that the earth's population is roughly 6.9 billion people and that an IQ is a gauge of intelligence determined by a person's knowledge in relation to his or her age.

If a piece of information does not meet these guidelines or if you are uncertain about whether it is common knowledge, always document the material.

Special Qualities of Source Materials

A more difficult problem than identifying common knowledge involves using an author's words and ideas improperly. Improper use often results from careless summarizing and paraphrasing. To use source materials without plagiarizing, learn to recognize their distinctive qualities.

Special qualities of sources

- **Distinctive prose style.** The author's chosen words, phrases, and sentence patterns.
- **Original facts.** Results of the author's personal research.
- **Personal interpretations of information.** The author's individual evaluation of his or her information.
- **Original ideas.** Ideas that are unique to a particular author.

As you work with sources, be aware of these distinguishing qualities and make certain that you do not incorporate into your writing the prose (word choices and sentence structures), original research, interpretations, or ideas of others without giving proper credit.

Consider, for example, the following paragraphs from Irvin Waller's (2011) *Rights for Victims of Crime: Rebalancing Justice* (Lanham, MD: Rowman).

Today, victims aren't the only ones who know about the pain, shock, humiliation, loss of control, and powerlessness that victims of crime experience at the hands of their offenders. A growing number of advocates and social scientists know only too well how feelings of anger, depression, worthlessness, and fear oscillate and reverberate over the weeks, months, years, and even decades following a victimizing incident. While law enforcement agents and judges may not be inclined to transfer their focus to the victim, many of these advocates and social scientists are experts in how to respond to victims in caring and just ways, and in some cases they even have solutions to stop victimization from happening in the future.

More often than not, we know how to provide emotional support and counseling to victims. We know how to protect the victim from the accused and how to give the victim a voice and power in the criminal justice system. We know how to inform victims of services that will help them and how to get them access to those services. We even know how to pay their mounting bills and how to stop much of the violence. In sum, we have the solutions as to how to put victims back in the center of our support, reparations, and justice systems. It's baffling, then, why governments are still not doing enough to apply this knowledge.

Now look at the following examples of faulty and acceptable summaries and paraphrases. Questionable phrases in the faulty samples are in red.

Faulty summary: plagiarism likely

Waller	Advocates

- People who support victims of violence understand that anger, depression, loss of self-worth, and worry last a long time following a victimizing incident.

- Enforcement agents and judges aren't always inclined to focus on victims.

p. 2

Acceptable summary: plagiarism unlikely

> Waller   Advocates
>
> – People who support victims of violence understand
>   that "feelings of anger, depression, worthlessness,
>   and fear oscillate and reverberate" long after a violent
>   experience.
>
> – Victims aren't always the chief concern of those in
>   the criminal justice system.
>
>   p. 2

Faulty paraphrase: plagiarism likely

> Waller   What we know
>
> – We know how to give emotional support and counseling
>   to support victims, how to protect victims and give
>   them power in the justice system, how to help them
>   find services and pay bills, and how to stop violence. In
>   other words, we can make victims central in our
>   support, payments, and justice system.
>
>   p. 2

Acceptable paraphrase (see page 21)

1h   Planning

After gathering information, organizing the research paper is an
exciting stage because you are ready to bring ideas together in a
clear and logical form.

Reviewing Notes

Begin by rereading the assignment sheet to reexamine the principles
guiding your work. Then review your notes to see the range of materials you have collected and to identify connections among ideas.

Acceptable paraphrase: plagiarism unlikely

Waller   What we know

– We know how to support victims emotionally and
  procedurally; we know how to protect them from
  future violence; we know how to ensure that they get
  the services they deserve. In other words, we already
  know how to make victims the focus of our efforts.

                                                    p. 2

Thesis Statement, Hypothesis, or Stated Objective

After rereading your notes, revise the thesis statement, hypothesis, or objective so that it accurately represents the paper you plan to write. Is the topic clear? Does it express your current (more informed) view? Does it contain appropriate qualifications and limitations? Is it worded effectively?

Organization

Having reread your materials and reconsidered your thesis or objective, plan the organization of your paper. Depending on the complexity of your paper, the requirements of your course, or your individual preferences, create either an informal outline (which is relatively simple and generally for your use only) or a formal outline (which is much more complex and generally intended for other readers). A complete discussion of both informal and formal outlines appears in Appendix B, section B8.

1i   Writing Strategies

Because incorporating research materials and using in-text documentation extend the time it takes to write a paper, allow ample time to write the draft of your paper. Consider both the general and special circumstances that affect the process of writing and revising any paper, as well as those issues that relate specifically to writing and revising a documented paper.

General Strategies for Drafting a Paper

Because the research paper is in many ways like all other papers, keep these general writing strategies in mind.

- **Gather materials.** Collect planning materials and writing supplies before you begin writing. Working consistently in the same location is also helpful because all materials are there when you wish to write.

- **Work from an outline.** Following an outline, whether informal or formal, develop paragraphs and sections; write troublesome sections late in the process.

- **Keep the paper's purpose in mind.** Arrange and develop only those ideas that your outline indicates are important.

- **Develop the paper "promised" by the thesis, hypothesis, or objective.** Incorporate only the ideas and information that support your thesis, hypothesis, or objective.

- **Attend to technical matters later.** Concentrate on developing your ideas and presenting your information; you can revise the paper later to correct any technical errors.

- **Rethink troublesome sections.** When sections are difficult to write, reconsider their importance or means of development. Revise the outline if necessary.

- **Reread as you write.** Reread early sections as you write to maintain a consistent tone and style.

- **Write alternative sections.** Write several versions of troublesome sections and then choose the best one.

- **Take periodic breaks.** Get away from your work for short periods so that you can maintain a fresh perspective and attain objectivity.

Strategies for Drafting a Research Paper

Because the research paper has its own distinct qualities and demands, keep these special strategies in mind.

- **Allow ample time.** Give yourself plenty of time to write a research paper; its length and complexity will affect the speed at which you work.

- **Think about sections, not paragraphs.** Think of the paper in terms of sections, not paragraphs. Large sections will probably contain several paragraphs.

- **Use transitions.** Although headings can divide your work into logical segments, use well-chosen transitional words to signal shifts between elements of the paper.

- **Attend to technical language.** Define technical terms carefully to clarify ideas.

- **Incorporate notes smoothly.** Use research materials to support and illustrate, not dominate, your discussion.

- **Document carefully.** Use in-text citations (notes in parentheses) to acknowledge the sources of your ideas and information (see Chapter 4, "Preparing the Reference List and In-Text Citations").

Questions for Revising Content

Examine the paper's content for clarity, coherence, and completeness. Consider these issues.

- **Title, introduction, headings, conclusion.** Are your title, introduction, headings, and conclusion well matched to the tone and purpose of the paper?

- **Thesis, hypothesis, or stated objective and development.** Does the thesis accurately represent your current view on the topic, and does the paper develop that idea? Does your paper develop in response to your hypothesis? Is the content of your paper matched to your stated objective?

- **Support for thesis, hypothesis, or stated objective.** Do research materials effectively support the paper's thesis, hypothesis, or stated objective? Have you eliminated materials (details, sentences, even paragraphs) that do not directly support your thesis, hypothesis, or stated objective?

- **Organization.** Does your organizational pattern present your ideas logically and effectively?

- **Use of materials.** Have you incorporated a range of materials to develop your ideas in a varied, interesting, and complete way?

- **Balance among sections.** Are the sections of the paper balanced in length and emphasis?

- **Balance among sources.** Have you used a variety of sources to support your ideas?

- **Transitions.** Do transitions connect sections of the paper in a coherent way?

Questions for Revising Style

Achieving coherent, balanced, well-developed content is one aspect of revision. Another consideration is achieving a clear and compelling presentation. Refine the paper's style, keeping these issues in mind.

- **Tone.** Is the tone suited to the topic and presentation?
- **Sentences.** Are the sentences varied in both length and type? Have you written active, rather than passive, sentences?
- **Diction.** Are the word choices vivid, accurate, and appropriate?
- **Introduction of research materials.** Have you introduced research materials (facts, summaries, paraphrases, and quotations) with variety and clarity?

Questions for Revising Technical Matters

Technical revision focuses on grammar, usage, punctuation, mechanics, spelling, and manuscript form. After revising content and style, consider technical revisions to make the presentation correct and precise, giving particular attention to issues related to documentation.

- **Grammar.** Are your sentences complete? Do pronouns agree in number and gender with their antecedents? Do verbs agree with their subjects? Have you worked to avoid errors that you commonly make?
- **Punctuation and mechanics.** Have you double-checked your punctuation? Have you spell-checked the paper? Have you used quotation marks and italics correctly?
- **Quotations.** Are quotations presented correctly, depending on their length or emphasis?
- **In-text citations.** Are in-text citations placed appropriately and punctuated correctly?
- **Reference list.** Have you listed only the sources actually used in the paper? Is your list alphabetized correctly? Is each entry complete and correct?
- **Manuscript guidelines.** Are margins, line spacing, and paging correct? Does the paper include all necessary elements?

APA style guidelines for manuscript preparation ensure that manuscripts follow uniform standards and, as a result, present the elements of papers in a generally understood way.

2a Parts of the Manuscript

A manuscript for an APA paper can contain as many as eight separate parts: the title page (with author note), an abstract, the text of the paper, a list of references, footnotes, tables, figures (with figure captions), and appendices. Not all papers have all of these elements, but when they do, they are arranged in this order.

The first part of this chapter addresses the specific requirements for preparing each element of an APA paper. The last part provides general manuscript guidelines.

Title Page

The first page of a manuscript is the title page (see pages 111 and 122 for samples), composed of the following elements.

- **Running head with paging.** As the first line of the title page, supply a running head—a shortened version of the paper's title typed in all capital letters—with the page number. Full instructions for creating the running head appear on page 35, and samples appear on pages 111–133.

- **Title.** Center the title and use headline-style capitalization (see page 47). A good title is descriptive, clarifying both the topic and the perspective of the paper; when possible, the title should create interest through effective wording. APA recommends that titles be no more than 12 words long (a title of this length generally fits on a single line). If the title is longer than one line, divide it logically and center both lines.

- **Author's name.** Two lines below the title, indicate your name (centered and capitalized normally); APA recommends using your first name and middle initial(s) for additional clarity. Two lines below your name, identify your affiliation; typically, this is your school's name, but you can indicate the city and state where you live. (Some instructors may also ask that you include the title of the course for which you wrote the paper.)

- **Author note.** At least four spaces below the affiliation, type the phrase *Author note* (not italicized but centered), followed by a series of clarifying paragraphs: (a) the first paragraph identifies the author's departmental and university affiliation; (b) the second paragraph identifies changes in affiliation, if any; (c) the third paragraph includes any necessary disclaimers or explanations of special circumstances, followed by acknowledgments; and (d) the fourth paragraph presents the author's contact information. Use separate, indented, double-spaced paragraphs for each element.

NOTE: Student work—papers for classes, theses, and dissertations—typically does not require an author note.

Parts of an APA Paper

- **Title page.** The opening page incorporates information to label the pages of the paper, highlights the title of the paper, and provides identifying information about the author. An author note may be included at the bottom of the title page.

- **Abstract.** This paragraph presents a brief but detailed overview of the paper, emphasizing key ideas and research procedures.

- **Text.** The text of an argumentative paper or review contains an introduction, body, and conclusion; it is frequently divided using headings that describe the main elements of the discussion. The text of a research study contains an introduction to the topic or problem (including a literature review), an explanation of methodology, a summary of results, and a discussion of the implications of the study.

- **Reference list.** The alphabetically arranged reference list provides publication information for the sources used in the paper.

- **Footnotes.** Content footnotes include clarifying discussions and explanations that might disrupt the flow of the paper. Alternatively, footnotes may be incorporated within the text of the paper using the footnote function of your word processor.

- **Tables.** Numbered tables include technical data in easily interpreted and comparable forms. References within the paper correspond to tables that appear on separate pages near the end of the manuscript.

- **Figures.** Visual images to support ideas in a paper (drawings, graphs, photographs, maps, and so on) appear as numbered figures. References within the paper correspond to the captioned figures that appear on separate pages at the end of the manuscript.

- **Appendices.** Appendices provide supplementary information that supports the ideas in the paper but would be awkward to include in the paper itself.

Abstract

The abstract (the second page of the manuscript) follows the title page and provides a brief description of the major ideas in the paper (see page 111 for a sample). Because it must summarize the full range of ideas and information in the paper, an abstract is generally written after the manuscript is complete. It must adhere to the following guidelines.

- **Heading.** Three lines below the running head, type the word *Abstract*, centered but not italicized. Two lines below, begin the paragraph.
- **Format.** The abstract is a single, unindented, double-spaced paragraph.
- **Length.** Abstracts in APA journals are typically 150 to 250 words.
- **Concision.** To save space in the abstract, use standard abbreviations (for example, *AMA* rather than *American Medical Association*); use digits for all numbers except those that begin sentences; and use active, rather than passive, voice. (See Appendix B, section B6.)
- **Content.** In the opening sentence, describe the topic or problem addressed in the paper. Use the remaining words in the paragraph to clarify methodology (for a research study), to identify four or five major ideas, and to explain results or conclusions. If a paper is lengthy and multifaceted, describe only the most important elements.
- **Keywords.** You may include a list of keywords with your abstract. Two lines below the abstract, indent, type *Keywords* (italicized, followed by a colon), and provide a brief list of words that best describe the content of your paper.

Text

The text of the paper begins on the third page of the manuscript (see pages 112–118 for sample pages). The running head, as always, appears on the top line. Three lines below, center the title, with headline-style capitalization but without special print features (bold, italics, underlining, change in font size, or quotation marks). Two lines below the title, the double-spaced paper begins. The organization of the body of the paper depends on the paper's focus.

An Argumentative Paper, Review, or Meta-Analysis

- **Introduction.** Define, describe, or clarify the topic (problem) and place it within its historical or scholarly context. Present a thesis (a statement of your topic and opinion) to clarify the purpose of your work.

- **Body.** Examine the facets of the topic (problem) by reviewing current research: evaluate the positions held by others; analyze current data; assess the interpretations of others; synthesize the information and ideas found in other people's work. Use headings and subheadings throughout this section to direct readers through your argument.

- **Conclusion.** Summarize key points, draw connections among important ideas, and reiterate your thesis.

- **Reference list.** In this labeled section, provide a list of sources cited in the paper (see Chapter 4).

- **Additional materials.** As appropriate, include the following labeled sections: footnotes, tables, figures, and appendices.

A Research Study

- **Introduction.** In this unlabeled section, describe the problem, state your hypothesis, and describe your research methodology. Consider the importance of the problem and the ways in which the study addresses the problem. Present a historical or contextual discussion of what scholars have written, acknowledging alternative perspectives and differing interpretations.

- **Method.** In this labeled section (further divided into labeled subsections), describe participants in the study (and procedures for selecting them), materials used (ranging from standard equipment to custom materials), and procedures (the step-by-step process for conducting the research).

- **Results.** In this labeled section, summarize the gathered information. It should be further subdivided into labeled subsections that analyze information that is illustrated by tables, figures, and other statistical material.

- **Discussion.** In this labeled section, make an assertion about the correlation of your data with your original hypothesis. The remaining discussion can address how your findings relate to the work of others, what qualifications are necessary, the value of alternative interpretations, or what conclusions you have reached. End the discussion by commenting on the significance of your research results.
- **Reference list.** In this labeled section, provide a list of sources cited in the paper (see Chapter 4).
- **Additional materials.** As appropriate, include the following labeled sections: footnotes, tables, figures, and appendices.

Reference List

The reference list, which continues the paging of the entire manuscript, provides publishing information for all sources used in the paper (see pages 119 and 130 for samples). Chapter 4 provides a comprehensive discussion of the information required in reference-list entries and the format for presenting the information. Chapters 5 through 8 provide explanations of 59 kinds of sources, with 124 separate samples for preparing reference-list entries for periodicals, books and other print materials, audiovisual sources, and electronic sources. Each entry appears with a corresponding in-text citation.

Footnotes

Content footnotes allow writers to provide additional discussion or clarification that, although important, might disrupt the flow of a paper.

Footnotes follow these guidelines for placement and presentation.

- **Heading.** Three lines below the running head, type the word *Footnotes*, centered but not italicized.
- **Order of notes.** On the footnote page, footnotes appear in the order in which references appear in the text of the paper. Double-check the numbering.
- **Format.** Footnotes are typed in paragraph style, double-spaced, with the first line indented and subsequent lines aligned at the left margin. "Tab" once (for a five-space indentation), insert the superscript number, and type the footnote. No space separates the note number from the first letter of the first word of the footnote.

- **Paging.** Footnotes appear on a new page. Multiple footnotes are placed on the same page, with no additional space between the notes.

NOTE: You may also incorporate footnotes within the text of the paper using the footnote function of your word-processing program.

Placing Note Numbers in the Paper

- **In-text notes.** Footnotes are numbered sequentially throughout a paper.

- **Placement of in-text note numbers.** In the text of the paper, refer to a content note by using a superscript number (a number placed above the line, like this[1]) without additional space. Word-processing programs allow you to achieve this result by using the "Font" feature.

- **Punctuation and note numbers.** Note numbers follow all punctuation marks, except dashes and parentheses. A note number precedes the dash[2]—without additional space. A note number may appear within parentheses (when it refers only to materials within the parentheses[3]). If the note refers to the entire sentence, however, it follows the parentheses (as in this sample).[4]

Tables

Because tables present labeled information in columns (vertical elements) and rows (horizontal elements) for easy interpretation or comparison, they are helpful additions to papers that use technical data (see page 132 for a sample). Within the text of the paper, a reference (for example, "See Table 1") directs readers to tables using numerals (which correspond to tables presented near the end of the manuscript). Tables are prepared on separate pages and are presented according to these principles.

- **Table identification.** Three lines below the running head (flush with the left margin), type the word *Table* and the table's Arabic numeral (Table 3, Table 4), not italicized.

- **Title of the table.** Two spaces below the table heading, also flush left, type the title of the table in italics, with headline-style capitalization. One line below, insert a horizontal, 1-point rule (line); use the graphics or "Insert" feature of your word-processing program to create this element.

- **Column headings.** Capitalize only the first letter of the first word of column headings, and center the column heading over the information in each column. One line below the column headings, insert a horizontal rule.

- **Parallel information and style.** To maintain consistency, headings should appear in parallel grammatical forms (all nouns, all gerunds, and so on), and numbers should appear in similar style (with decimals, rounded to whole numbers, and so on).

- **Spacing.** The primary elements of tables are single-spaced, and columns should be separated by at least three spaces for visual clarity. However, table notes (general and specific) are double-spaced.

- **Repeated information.** If information from a table extends beyond one page, repeat the column headings.

- **Table notes (general).** To provide an explanation of an entire table, include a general note. One line below the body of the table, insert a horizontal rule. Below the rule, type the word *Note* (italicized and flush with the left margin) followed by a period; after one space, type the text of the note, which remains flush left if it extends beyond one line. Place a period at the end of the note, even if it is not a complete sentence. These notes are double-spaced.

- **Table notes (specific).** To provide an explanation of a specific element within a table, include a specific note. Within the table, insert a superscript lowercase letter—like this[a]— following the element. One line below the body of the table, insert a horizontal rule. Below the horizontal rule and flush with the left margin, insert the corresponding superscript lowercase letter, followed by the explanation. Place a period at the end of the note, even if it is not a complete sentence. If a table also has a general table note, it appears first; the specific table note appears on the line below. If a table has two or more specific notes, they continue on the same line, separated by one space. These notes are double-spaced.

- **Paging.** Each table must begin on a new page.

Figures

Figures are visual elements—drawings, graphs, photographs, maps, and so on—that cannot be reproduced by traditional typing (see page 132 for a sample). Each figure is numbered as it is used in the paper; original figures then appear on separate pages at the end of the manuscript, following these guidelines.

- **Figure.** Three lines below the running head, insert the figure in the highest quality possible, with sharp contrast in photographs, distinct shading in bar graphs, and clear lettering in line graphs. Figures must be scaled to fit appropriately on the page.

- **Label.** Below the figure, flush left, type the word *Figure*, the number of the figure, and a period (*Figure 1, Figure 2*). All of these elements are italicized.

- **Caption.** One space after the figure label, type the caption, using sentence-style capitalization. Place a period at the end of the caption, even if it is not a complete sentence. The caption is *not* italicized.

- **Spacing and indentation.** Figure captions are double-spaced. If a caption extends beyond one line, it continues flush left.

- **Fonts.** Printed text that is part of a figure—labels, for example—should use a sans-serif font such as Helvetica. The minimum acceptable font size is 8 points, with 14 points being the maximum.

- **Paging.** Each figure must be presented on a separate page.

Special Concerns for Figures

- **Value of the figure.** Consider whether the figure presents information more effectively than would a textual discussion or a table. Because figures are more difficult to prepare than print-based elements, make sure that your time is well spent in creating one.

- **Computer-generated figures.** Today's word-processing programs are capable of creating a wide range of figures, including bar graphs, line graphs, and pie charts. Allow sufficient time to familiarize yourself with the procedures for creating a figure.

- **Visual clutter.** Include only figures that highlight important elements of your discussion. To achieve this goal, eliminate all extraneous detail in graphs, charts, and drawings and crop (trim) photographs and maps to focus visual attention on key features, not superficial or unrelated elements.

- **Visual clarity.** To ensure that figures achieve maximum impact, make sure that the print quality of graphs and charts is high (best achieved by laser printing). Furthermore, make sure that bar charts, photographs, and maps are sharply focused and have clear tonal contrast.

Appendices

One or more appendices can follow figures and continue the page numbering of the entire manuscript. Each appendix should adhere to the following guidelines.

- **Heading.** Three lines below the running head, type the word *Appendix*, centered but not italicized. If more than one appendix is included, label each one with a letter (Appendix A, Appendix B).

- **Appendix title.** Two lines below the heading, type the title of the appendix, centered, with headline-style capitalization.

- **Text.** Begin the text two lines below the appendix title; appended material is double-spaced.

- **Paging.** Each appendix begins on a new page.

2b   General Manuscript Guidelines

In preparing a paper in APA style, writers must conform to a variety of principles, each of which is described in the following sections.

Paper

Use heavy-weight, white bond, 8½" × 11" paper. Avoid lightweight paper because it does not hold up well under review or grading.

Font Selection

Fonts—designed versions of letters, numbers, and characters—appear in different sizes, referred to as *points*. APA encourages the use of serif fonts (those with cross marks on individual letters) for the text of the paper; Times New Roman is the preferred font. Sans-serif fonts (those without cross marks) such as Century Gothic or Tahoma may be used to label figures and illustrations. Font sizes for all elements of the paper except figures should be 12 points, the default size in most word-processing programs. (*NOTE:* Within figures, APA allows fonts from 8 to 14 points.)

Font Sizes, Fonts, and Their Uses

FONT SIZE	SERIF	SANS-SERIF	USES
8 pt.		Tahoma	Figures
12 pt.	Times New Roman		Primary text and supporting materials
14 pt.		Century Gothic	Figures

Use italics (*slanted type*), not underlining, in all parts of your paper. Use your word-processing program's capabilities to insert accents, diacritical marks, and symbols directly in your paper, rather than adding them by hand.

Line Spacing

Double-space all parts of the paper except elements within tables and figures, which use single-spacing. For visual clarity, you may triple- or quadruple-space before or after equations or other visual elements. (*NOTE:* Three lines separate the running head from the elements of the paper.)

Word Spacing

Use two spaces after periods, question marks, and exclamation points (end punctuation). Use one space after commas, colons, and semicolons (internal punctuation); periods with initials (E. V. Debbs); and between elements in citations. No space is required with periods in abbreviations (p.m., e.g., U.S.), with hyphens (first-year student), or with dashes (example: The sounds of vowels—*a, e, i, o, u*—must be transcribed carefully to record speech accurately).

Margins and Indentations

Leave 1-inch margins at the left, right, top, and bottom of each page. If the "default" margins for your word-processing program are not 1 inch, reset them to 1 inch. Do not justify the right margin (that is, create a straight text edge on the right); instead, use left justification, which aligns the text on the left but leaves the right margin irregular (ragged). Do not hyphenate words at the ends of lines.

A five- to seven-space indentation (½ inch)—best achieved by using the "Tab" feature—is required at the beginning of paragraphs and for the first line of footnotes. The continuous indentation that is required for long quotations and for second and subsequent lines of reference-list entries is best achieved by using the "Indent" feature.

Seriation

To indicate a series or a sequence within a prose paragraph, enclose lowercase letters in parentheses. Although this pattern should not be overused, it has two advantages: (a) It provides visual clarity, and (b) it makes a long sentence with multiple elements easily readable. To achieve a similar effect with a series of set-off sentences or paragraphs, use Arabic numerals followed by periods.

1. Indent the number five to seven spaces from the margin (½ inch).

2. After a period and one space, type the word, phrase, sentence, or paragraph.

3. If the item continues beyond one line, subsequent lines can be flush left or indented.

When elements are not presented in chronological order or by order of importance, they may be set off using bullets (typically filled circles or squares).

- This pattern draws attention to each element.
- The order of elements is deemphasized.
- Indentation patterns are the same as for numbered lists.

Paging (Running Head)

On the first line of the title page, flush left, type the words *Running head* (not italicized, but followed by a colon). After one space, type an abbreviated version of the title of the paper in all capital letters; it can contain no more than 50 characters (letters, numbers, symbols, punctuation, and spaces). On the same line, flush right, insert the page number. This information (label, title, and page number) must be at least one-half inch from the top of the page; the text begins three lines below the running head (see pages 111 and 122 for samples). On subsequent pages of the paper, use only the running head itself and the page number, omitting the label *Running head* (see pages 112 and 123 for samples).

Use the "Header" feature of your word processing program to type the running head and use codes to insert page numbers automatically throughout the document.

Headings for Sections

Use headings to divide and subdivide the paper into logical, and sometimes sequential, sections. APA establishes five potential levels of division for manuscripts, while acknowledging that most writing does not require the use of all five.

- **Level-1 headings** are centered, with headline-style capitalization and boldface type.
- **Level-2 headings** are flush left, with headline-style capitalization and boldface type.
- **Level-3 headings** are indented, with sentence-style capitalization, boldface type, and a period.

- **Level-4 headings** are indented, with sentence-style capitalization, boldface italic type, and a period.
- **Level-5 headings** are indented, with sentence-style capitalization, italic type, and a period.

One level of division

Level-1 Heading

Two levels of division

Level-1 Heading

Level-2 Heading

Three levels of division

Level-1 Heading

Level-2 Heading

  Level-3 Heading.

Four levels of division

Level-1 Heading

Level-2 Heading

  Level-3 Heading.

  Level-4 heading.

Five levels of division

Level-1 Heading

Level-2 Heading

  Level-3 Heading.

  Level-4 heading.

  Level-5 heading.

When new headings are required, do not begin new pages. Simply type the new heading two lines below the last line of the preceding paragraph.

Submitting the Paper

Submit manuscripts according to your instructor's guidelines, acknowledging that alternative formats exist.

- **Paper.** Secure the pages with a paper clip in the upper-left corner and place them in a manila envelope with your name and affiliation typed or written on the outside. Save a copy of the file on your computer.

- **Flash drive.** Submit a copy of the final paper on a flash drive, clearly labeled with your name and affiliation, as well as a note about the word-processing program you used. Save a copy of the file on your computer.

- **Electronic.** Attach the file version of the paper to an e-mail with a clear subject line (Paper 4: Test Anxiety), as well as a note about the word-processing program you used. If you do not receive confirmation of delivery, resubmit the e-mail and attachment. Print a copy of your e-mail as a record.

Generally, APA style follows conventions that need little explanation (for example, periods follow sentences that make statements, and question marks follow sentences that pose questions). However, in some situations, agreement about editorial issues is not universal. (Should commas separate *all* elements of listed items? Are prepositions in titles capitalized?) In such special circumstances, follow the APA guidelines in this chapter to ensure that your manuscript meets expectations.

3a   Punctuation and Mechanics

Periods

Periods most often serve as end punctuation (after sentences), but they are also used with abbreviations and in other specialized contexts.

USES OF PERIODS	EXAMPLES
End of a complete sentence	Periods end most sentences.
Initials with an author's name	C. S. Lewis
Reference-list abbreviations	Ed., Vol. 6, pp. 34–38, Rev. ed.
After figure captions	*Figure 3.* Student use of computers.
Latin abbreviations	i.e., e.g., vs., p.m.
U.S. when used as an adjective	U.S. government, U.S. economy
Abbreviation for inch	in. (distinct from the preposition *in*)
Decimal points in fractions	2.45 ml, 33.5 lb

Commas

Commas are internal forms of punctuation, most often used to separate elements within sentences. However, they also serve a few other purposes.

USES OF COMMAS	EXAMPLES
Three or more items in a series	men, women, and children
Set off nonessential information	The room, which was well lighted, was on the south corridor.
Clauses of a compound sentence	The first survey was a failure, but the second one was a success.
Years with exact dates	May 25, 2011, the experiment began. *But* May 2011, the experiment began.
Years within in-text citations	(Armstrong, 2012); (Romines, 2010)
Numbers of 1,000 or larger	11,205 students, 1,934 books (see "Number Style," pages 50–51, for exceptions)

Semicolons

In APA style, semicolons serve two purposes, one related to compound sentences and one related to elements in a series.

USES OF SEMICOLONS	EXAMPLES
Join clauses of a compound sentence when no coordinating conjunction is used	Females responded positively; males responded negatively.
Separate elements in a series when the elements contain commas	The test groups were from Fresno, California; St. Louis, Missouri; and Raleigh, North Carolina.

Colons

Colons serve six distinct purposes in APA style. A complete sentence must precede the colon, and if the explanatory material that follows a colon is a complete sentence, the first word is capitalized.

USES OF COLONS	EXAMPLES
Introduce a phrase that serves as an explanation or illustration	Two words triggered the strongest reactions: *preferential* and *special*.

USES OF COLONS	EXAMPLES
Introduce a sentence that serves as an explanation or illustration (the first word of the clarifying sentence is capitalized)	The responses were quickly summarized: Patients were dissatisfied.
Separate the title from the subtitle (the first word of the subtitle is capitalized)	*Decoding Delinquency: Psychological and Social Factors That Influence Youth Behavior*
Separate elements in a ratio	The ratio was 3:10.
Separate the place of publication and publisher in a reference list entry	Didion, J. (2005). *The year of magical thinking*. New York, NY: Vintage Books.
Separate the numbered section and page number in a reference-list entry for a newspaper	Page, C. (2010, April 16). One very big thumbs down. *The Chicago Tribune*, p. 1:19.

Dashes

Formed by typing two hyphens (with no spaces before and after) or using the em-dash feature of your word-processing program, dashes serve a few selected purposes; however, they should be used sparingly in academic writing. Also note that if a title contains a dash, the word that follows the dash is capitalized.

USES OF DASHES	EXAMPLES
Indicate a break in the thought of the sentence	The national heritage of participants—they identified themselves—proved less important than researchers anticipated.
Insert a series of elements that contain commas	Universities in two small cities—Terre Haute, Indiana, and Bloomington, Illinois—offer similar programs in psychology.

The shorter and more specialized en dash, which can be inserted using your word-processing program, is used to indicate inclusive pages in reference-list entries and in-text citations (pp. 102–133, pp. 435–436) and to show equal weight in a compound modifier (parent–teacher conference, doctor–patient relationship).

Hyphens

Hyphens are most often used to join compound words that precede the noun they modify; this pattern ensures that modification is clear in individual sentences (example: First-person narratives are seldom suitable in academic writing). When the modifiers follow the noun, they are generally written without hyphens (example: The opening paragraph was written in the first person). When general usage determines that a compound has become a permanent part of the language, it may be spelled either open (high school) or closed (casebook); consult a collegiate dictionary for individual cases.

USES OF HYPHENS	EXAMPLES
A compound that functions as an adjective	high-risk behaviors, time-intensive work, all-or-nothing approach
A compound with a number that functions as an adjective	two-part explanation, sixth-grade teacher, 50-word paragraph
A compound using the prefix *self-*	self-help books, self-inflicted injuries, self-imposed limitations
A compound that could be misread	re-form ("form again," not "change"), re-mark ("mark again," not "comment"), re-count ("count again," not "remember")
A compound using a prefix when the base word is capitalized	anti-American sentiment, pseudo-Freudian interpretation, post-Depression regulations
A compound using a prefix when the base word is a number	pre-1960s complacency, post-2010 requirements
A compound using a prefix when the base word is more than one word	non-user-friendly instructions, anti-off-site testing, non-peer-reviewed journals
A fraction used as an adjective	three-fourths majority
A prefix that ends with the first letter of the base word (except e)	anti-inflammatory drug, post-traumatic stress (but preexisting condition)

SPECIAL CASES—NO HYPHENATION	EXAMPLES
A compound with an adverb ending in -ly	newly designed test, recently certified teacher, uncharacteristically exaggerated statement
A compound with a comparative or superlative adjective	less capable practitioner, clearer written instructions, most egregious error
A foreign phrase used as a modifier	ad hoc committee, a priori reasoning, laissez faire attitude
A common fraction used as a noun	two thirds of students, one half of the sample, one quarter of the residents

Quotation Marks

Quotation marks are used within the text of a paper to identify titles of brief works, to indicate a quotation containing fewer than 40 words, and to highlight words used in special ways.
NOTE: Quotation marks are not used in reference-list entries, and quotations of more than 40 words are indented and use no quotation marks. (See section 4f for additional information on quoted material.)

USES OF QUOTATION MARKS	EXAMPLES
Titles of chapters, articles, songs, subsites of websites, and so on (quotation marks are used in the text only; reference-list entries *do not* use quotation marks)	"The High-Risk Child" (chapter), "Grant Writing vs. Grant Getting" (article), "My Vietnam" (song), "Adlerian Web Links" (subsite)
Quoted material (written or spoken) of fewer than 40 words when used word for word	Duncan (2010) asserted, "Normative behavior is difficult to define because community standards apply" (p. 233).
Words used counter to their intended meaning (irony, slang, or coined usage)	Her "abnormal" behavior was, in fact, quite normal.

Parentheses

Parentheses are used, always in pairs, to separate information and elements from the rest of the sentence.

USES OF PARENTHESES	EXAMPLES
Set off clarifying information	We provided parents with four samples (see Figures 1–4).
Set off publication dates in in-text summaries	Wagner (2010) noted that special-needs students responded well to the protocol.
Set off parenthetical references within the text; they must correspond to entries in the reference list	First-time offenders are more likely to respond to group therapy sessions than are repeat offenders (Gillum & Sparks, 2011).
Set off page references that follow direct quotations	Sanchez (2012) noted, "Self-concept is an intangible quality among immigrant children" (p. 34).
Introduce an abbreviation to be used in place of a full name in subsequent sections of a paper	The American Psychological Association (APA) published its first guidelines for manuscript preparation in 1929. Since then, APA has updated its guidelines eight times.
Set off letters that indicate divisions or sequences within paragraphs	The test included sections on (a) vocabulary, (b) reading comprehension, and (c) inferences.

Brackets

Brackets are used within parentheses or quotation marks to provide clarifying information. Use brackets sparingly because they can become distracting in academic writing.

USES OF BRACKETS	EXAMPLES
Clarifying information in a quotation	Thompson (2010) observed, "When [students] work in groups, they perform better" (p. 11). (Used to replace *they* in the original text.)

USES OF BRACKETS	EXAMPLES
Parenthetical information already in parentheses	(See Figure 4 [Percentages of students with learning disabilities] for more details.)
Clarifying information in a reference-list entry	*Eternal sunshine of the spotless mind* [Motion picture].
Indicate an editorial note	Bailey (2012) noted that "family members *and* [italics mine] friends must agree to support a patient's recovery plan" (p. 219).

Slashes

Slashes serve very specialized functions, often related to the presentation of compounds, comparisons, and correlations.

USES OF SLASHES	EXAMPLES
Hyphenated compounds in alternatives	first-day/second-day experiences
Fractions (numerator/denominator)	3/4, X + Y/Z
Represent *per* in units with a numerical value	0.7 ml/L
Indicate phonemes in English	/b/
Separate dual publication dates for reprinted works	Hirsch (1999/2009)

Capitalization

APA follows universally accepted patterns for most capitalization. However, APA uses two distinct capitalization patterns for titles—headline style and sentence style—depending on whether they appear in the text of the paper or in the reference list.

USES OF CAPITALIZATION	EXAMPLES
Proper nouns and proper adjectives	Jean Piaget, Robert Coles, Chinese students, Elizabethan drama

continued on next page

USES OF CAPITALIZATION	EXAMPLES
Specific departments (and academic units) in universities and specific courses	Department of Psychology, Indiana State University, Criminology 235
Trade and brand names	Prozac, Xerox, WordPerfect 12.0
Titles of articles or parts of books in the text: Use headline-style capitalization.	"The Middle-Child Syndrome," "Family Dynamics in a Changing World"
Nouns used with numbers or letters in describing sequenced methods or examples	Day 4, Experiment 6, Table 1, *Figure 3*
Formal titles of tests	Scholastic Aptitude Test
Table titles: Use headline-style capitalization.	*Grade Ranges of Remedial Students*
First word of a sentence that follows a colon	One challenge could not be met: The cost of the procedure was too great.
Running head (all capitals)	BEYOND BIRTH ORDER, TEST QUESTIONS

SPECIAL CASES—NO CAPITALIZATION	EXAMPLES
General references to departments and courses	a number of departments of sociology, a speech pathology course
Figure captions: Use sentence-style capitalization.	*Figure 1*. Percentages of international students by country of origin.
Generic or scientific names of drugs or ingredients	fluoxetine hydrochloride (*but* Prozac)
General titles of tests	an achievement test

Capitalization of Titles

APA follows two distinct patterns for the capitalization of titles: one within the text of a paper and one in the reference list and other supporting pages.

- **In-text capitalization.** In the text of a paper, both in your prose and in in-text citations (parenthetical notes), use headline-style capitalization, no matter what kind of source you use.
- **Reference-list (and other) capitalization.** In the reference list, only periodical titles use headline-style capitalization. The titles of articles and all other sources (such as books or motion pictures) use sentence-style capitalization.
- **Capitalization of special in-text elements.** Headline-style capitalization is used for titles of tables.

Article Title in the Text

In "Partners in Treatment: Relational Psychoanalysis and Harm Reduction Therapy," Rothschild (2010) described and analyzed two approaches to the treatment of at-risk patients, as well as advocated for efforts to integrate their techniques.

Article Title in a Reference-List Entry

Rothschild, D. (2010). Partners in treatment: Relational psychoanalysis and harm reduction therapy. *Journal of Clinical Psychology, 66,* 136–149.

Book Title in the Text

In *The Mismeasure of Man,* Gould (1981) provided useful insights into the ethical and unethical uses to which intelligence tests can be put.

Book Title in a Reference-List Entry

Gould, S. J. (1981). *The mismeasure of man.* New York, NY: Norton.

NOTE: The running head of your written work appears in all capital letters.

Headline-Style Capitalization

GUIDING PRINCIPLES	EXAMPLES
Capitalize the first and last word; capitalize all other words except articles, *to* (as part of an infinitive phrase), and conjunctions or prepositions of three or fewer letters.	Edwards's *Post-Operative Stress: A Guide for the Family,* "Agent of Change: The Educational Legacy of Thomas Dewey"

Sentence-Style Capitalization

GUIDING PRINCIPLES	EXAMPLES
Capitalize the first word of a title or subtitle; otherwise, capitalize only proper nouns and proper adjectives.	Edwards's *Post-operative stress: A guide for the family*, "Agent of change: The educational legacy of Thomas Dewey"

Italics

APA requires the use of italics (slanted fonts, as in *this example*), rather than underlining, in computer-generated manuscripts.

USES OF ITALICS	EXAMPLES
Titles of full-length works: periodicals, books, motion pictures, CDs, websites, and so on	*Journal of Cognitive Psychology* (journal), *Wordplay and Language Learning* (book), *A Beautiful Mind* (motion picture), *Back to Black* (CD), *WebMD* (website)
Genus, species, or varieties	*Pan troglodytes verus* (common chimpanzee)
New terms (when introduced and defined; thereafter, presented without italics)	The term *Nisei*, meaning second-generation Japanese Americans
Words, letters, or phrases used as words, letters, or phrases	Different impressions are created by the words *small, diminutive, minute,* and *tiny.*
Words that could be misread	*more* specific detail (meaning additional detail that is specific)
Letters used as symbols or algebraic variables	$IQ = \dfrac{MA \text{ (mental age)}}{CA \text{ (chronological age)}} \times 100$
Titles of tables	*Factors That Influence School Choice*
Volume numbers for periodicals (in reference-list entries)	*American Journal of Nursing, 112; Developmental Psychology, 48*
Anchors for scales	Satisfaction ratings ranged from 1 (*very satisfied*) to 8 (*very dissatisfied*).

Number Style

In APA style, numerals are used more frequently than words, whether in written texts or supporting materials; Arabic numerals are preferred in an APA-style text, rather than Roman numerals.

USES OF NUMERALS	EXAMPLES
Numbers of 10 and larger	14 respondents, 26 chapters, 11th article
Numbers smaller than 10 when compared with numbers larger than 10	the 4th chapter of 20; 2 of 30 research subjects; 13 sources, including 10 articles and 3 books
Numbers preceding units of measurement	6-in. mark, 300-mg capsule
Numbers used statistically or mathematically	7.5 of respondents, a ratio of 5:2, 9% of the sample, the 3rd percentile
Numbers that represent periods of time	6 years, 5 months, 1 week, 3 hours, 15 minutes, 7:15 p.m.
Numbers that represent dates	November 1, 2011; April 15, 2012
Numbers that represent ages	4-year-olds, students who are 8 years old
Numbers for population size	1 million citizens
Numbers that refer to participants or subjects	7 participants, 4 rhesus monkeys
Numbers that refer to points or scores on a scale	a score of 6.5 on an 8-point scale
Numbers for exact sums of money	a DVD costing $24.25, a $35 fee
Numbers used as numbers	a scale ranging from 1 to 5
Numbers that indicate placement in a series	Exam 4, Figure 9
Numbers for parts of books	Chapter 2, page 6

continued on next page

USES OF NUMERALS	EXAMPLES
Numbers in a list of four or more numbers	The sample was composed of work groups with 2, 4, 6, and 8 members.
Numbers in the abstract for a paper	All numbers appear in numeral form.

USES OF WORDS FOR NUMBERS	EXAMPLES
Numbers smaller than 10 (see exceptions in the previous table)	two experimental models, three lists, a one-topic discussion
Zero and one (when confusion is likely)	zero-percent increase, one-unit design
Numbers that begin sentences	Sixteen authors contributed to the collection. Thirteen people attended.
Numbers that begin titles	"Twelve Common Errors in Research," *Seven-Point Scales: Values and Limitations*
Numbers that begin headings	*Five Common Income Groups* (table heading)
Numbers in common fractions	two thirds of teachers, a reduction of three fourths
Numbers in common names and phrases	the Seven Deadly Sins, the Ten Commandments, the Seven Wonders of the World

Cardinal and Ordinal Numbers

Cardinal numbers (one, two, three, and so on) indicate quantity; ordinal numbers (first, second, third, and so on) indicate order. The principles described in the preceding tables apply whether the numbers are cardinal or ordinal.

Commas in Numbers

In most writing contexts, commas are used in numbers of 1,000 or larger. Place commas between groups of three digits, moving from the right. However, in the following situations, commas are not used.

NUMBERS WITHOUT COMMAS	EXAMPLES
Page numbers	page 1287, pages 1002–1021, (p. 1349)
Degrees of temperature	2044°F
Serial numbers	033776901
Binary digits	01100100
Numbers to the right of decimal points	2.09986
Designations of acoustical frequency	1000 Hz
Degrees of freedom	$F(31, 1000)$

Plurals of Numbers

Whether numbers are presented as numerals or words, form their plurals by adding only s or *es:* 1960s, threes, sixes, 25s. Do not use apostrophes to indicate plurality.

Numbered Seriation

To indicate series, sequences, or alternatives in a series of set-off sentences or paragraphs, use Arabic numerals, followed by periods (see pages 34–35).

3b General Style

The way in which a manuscript is written affects the ways in which readers respond. A well-written paper communicates ideas efficiently and effectively, whereas a poorly written paper distracts readers from its central ideas. Therefore, take time to revise your writing to improve its presentation, paying special attention to elements that improve the effectiveness of communication.

Transitions

Transitions—words or phrases that signal relationships among elements of your writing—facilitate readers' progress through a paper. Use transitional words and phrases to create appropriate links within your work.

Transitional Words and Phrases

RELATIONSHIP	EXAMPLES
Addition	also, and, besides, equally, further, furthermore, in addition, moreover, next, too
Similarity	also, likewise, moreover, similarly
Difference	but, however, in contrast, nevertheless, on the contrary, on the other hand, yet
Examples	for example, for instance, in fact, specifically, to illustrate
Restatements	finally, in brief, in conclusion, in other words, in short, in summary, on the whole, that is, therefore, to sum up
Results	accordingly, as a result, consequently, for this reason, so, therefore, thereupon, thus
Chronology	after, afterward, before, during, earlier, finally, first, immediately, in the meantime, later, meanwhile, next, second, simultaneously, soon, still, then, third, when, while
Location	above, below, beyond, farther, here, nearby, opposite, there, to the left, to the right, under

Verb Tense

Verbs are primary communicators in sentences, signaling action (*organized, summarized, presented*) or indicating a state of being (*seemed, was*). Well-chosen, specific verbs make writing direct and forceful. Moreover, tenses of verbs indicate chronology, clarifying the time relationships that you want to express.

In APA style, verbs are used in specific ways to signal ideas clearly.

USES OF VERBS	EXAMPLES
Active voice (to clarify who is doing what)	Respondents completed the questionnaire in 15 minutes. (*Not:* The questionnaire was completed in 15 minutes by the respondents.)

USES OF VERBS	EXAMPLES
Passive voice (to clarify who or what received the action, not the person or people responsible)	Traditional IQ tests were administered as part of the admissions process. (The use of the tests is emphasized, not the givers of the tests.)
Past tense (to place an action in the past or to describe previous research)	Bradshaw and Hines (2012) summarized their results in one incisive paragraph.
Present perfect tense (to describe an action that began in the past and continues to the present or to describe a concept with continued application)	In the years since, researchers have incorporated Piaget's methods in a variety of studies of children.
Subjunctive mood (to describe a conditional situation or one contrary to fact)	If the sampling were larger, the results might be different.

Agreement

Agreement is the matching of words or word forms according to number (singular and plural) and gender (masculine, feminine, or neuter). Verbs take singular or plural forms depending on whether their subjects are singular or plural.

Subject–Verb Agreement

SPECIAL CIRCUMSTANCES	EXAMPLES
Foreign words—*datum* (singular) versus *data* (plural), *phenomenon* (singular) versus *phenomena* (plural), and others: Choose the correct form.	The data suggest that our preconceptions were ill founded. (plural subject/plural verb) The phenomenon is unlikely to occur again. (singular subject/singular verb)
Collective (or group) nouns: Consider whether members of the group act in unison (singular) or individually (plural).	The couple initiates the counseling sessions. (singular meaning to stress shared action) The couple meet separately with the counselor. (plural meaning to stress separate actions)

continued on next page

SPECIAL CIRCUMSTANCES	EXAMPLES
Singular and plural subjects joined by *or* or *nor*: Match the verb to the nearer subject.	Neither the parents nor the therapist finds their meetings helpful. Or: Neither the therapist nor the parents find their meetings helpful.

Pronouns must match their antecedents (the words to which they refer) in both number and gender.

Pronoun–Antecedent Agreement

COMMON CIRCUMSTANCES	EXAMPLES
Agreement in number: Match the pronoun to its antecedent. (*Also see* "Biased Language," pages 56–58.)	A participant secures his or her stipend from the controller's office. (singular) Participants secure their stipends from the controller's office. (plural)
Agreement in gender: Match the pronoun to the antecedent. (*Also see* "Biased Language.")	Devon was the first student to complete his exam. (masculine) The lab rat (subject 3) stopped eating its food during the experiment. (neuter)
Who and *whom*: Use *who* in a subject position; use *whom* in an object position.	Who is responsible for compiling the data? (subject: *He* or *she* is.) To whom should we address our inquiries? (object: Address inquiries to *him* or *her*.)

Parallelism

Parallelism is the use of equivalent forms when words are used together: nouns, verbs of the same tense or form, and so on.

PARALLELS	EXAMPLES
Elements in a series: Use matching forms.	Even young children are expected to add, to subtract, and to multiply. (parallel verb forms) Reading, writing, speaking, listening, and thinking compose the language arts. (parallel gerund/noun forms)

PARALLELS	EXAMPLES
Correlative conjunctions (*both/ and, either/or, neither/ nor, not only/but also*): Use matching forms of the words, phrases, and clauses that are linked.	The youngest child in a large family is either the most independent or the least independent of the siblings. (parallel phrases) We found not only that the experiment was too costly but also that it was too time consuming. (parallel clauses)

3c Word Choice

Word choice makes meaning clear to readers. Specific word choices affect the tone of writing—implying your perception of yourself, your readers, your subject, and your purpose in writing. Consequently, choose words carefully to communicate ideas effectively.

Noun Clusters

Noun clusters are created when nouns, often in multiples, are used to modify yet another noun. Although the modification patterns may be grammatically correct (nouns *can* function as modifiers), they often create dense clusters of meaning that have to be sorted through carefully.

For example, the phrase *first-year student success ensurance initiative* is overly long, does not read smoothly, and has to be deconstructed. To improve readability, untangle the nouns and place them in easily readable phrases: *an initiative to ensure the success of first-year students.* The reconstructed phrase is easier to interpret than the original and, therefore, communicates the idea more efficiently than does the original.

Jargon

Jargon is the specialized language of a professional group. In some instances, a specific technical term communicates an idea more efficiently than an explanation in everyday language. For instance, the phrase *correlational analyses* explains in two generally understood words a process by which data are both systematically linked and logically compared. However, in many instances, common language that is well selected communicates ideas in a more straightforward and less pretentious way than jargon does. For example, in many instances the phrase *classroom teacher* communicates an idea with greater clarity and less distraction than the more affected phrase *teacher/practitioner,* which is a stilted way of expressing an idea that is implicit in the word *teacher.*

In your writing, choose words with care. Use technical jargon only when it communicates ideas clearly and efficiently—that is, when it is precise and helpful. Never use jargon to impress, because an over-reliance on technical terms (especially those that do not communicate ideas precisely and quickly) frustrates readers and clutters prose.

Colloquialisms

In academic writing, avoid colloquialisms—expressions that are better suited for conversation and other forms of informal communication. Words and phrases such as *write-up* (instead of *report*), *only a few* (rather than 7%), or *get-together* (in place of *meeting* or *colloquium*) not only lack the specificity of more technical, formal language but also suggest a lack of precision that may make readers question the care with which you have described your research. For these reasons, use precise, professional language in your writing.

Specificity

Choose specific words to create clear meaning; do not assume that readers will infer meaning from vague language. For example, rather than writing that a survey contained *numerous questions,* be specific and indicate that it contained *45 questions.* Instead of noting that a study was based on the responses of *many Midwestern students,* describe the research group more precisely: *2,000 first-year college students in Missouri and Iowa.* Even this description could be made more specific by noting the percentage of male/female respondents, the kinds of schools (liberal arts colleges, small state universities, large state universities, and so on), and the locations of the schools (urban, rural, and so on).

The credibility of research depends on using language that communicates clearly. Consequently, choose words that are as specific as possible.

Biased Language

Whether employed consciously or unconsciously, the use of biased language conveys a writer's insensitivity, ignorance, or, in some instances, prejudice—any of which disrupts communication because readers expect to find balance and fairness in what they read. Writing that incorporates biased language reflects badly on the writer, alienates thoughtful readers, and consequently interferes with effective communication.

As a writer, you should make a conscious effort to use accurate, equitable language. Recognizing that your potential readers represent a broad spectrum of society, choose words with care and avoid stereotypes.

Racial and Ethnic Bias

Language that is racially and ethnically biased often relies on dated words related to racial or ethnic groups. In other instances, racially and ethnically biased word choices ignore the distinct groups that exist within larger classifications, thereby perpetuating broad stereotypes. Consequently, it is preferable to refer to racial or ethnic groups as specifically as possible.

Preferred Racial or Ethnic Terms

QUESTIONABLE	PREFERRED TERMS FOR AMERICAN CITIZENS	PREFERRED TERMS FOR NON-AMERICAN CITIZENS
Arab	Arab American; or Saudi American, Iraqi American, and so on	Saudi, Iraqi, Afghan, and so on
Hispanic	Latino/Latina, Chicano/Chicana; or Cuban American, and so on	Mexican, Cuban, Costa Rican, and so on
Indian	Native American; or Cherokee, Ogallal Sioux, Seminole, and so on	Mesoamerican, Inuit, and so on
Black	African American; or Kenyan American, and so on	African; or Ugandan, Kenyan, and so on
White	European American; or Italian American, French American, Irish American, and so on	Caucasian, European; or German, French, Hungarian, Russian, and so on
Oriental	Asian American; or Japanese American, Korean American, Chinese American, and so on	Asian; or Korean, Japanese, Vietnamese, and so on

Gender Bias

Language based on stereotypical gender roles—also called sexist language—implies through choices of nouns, pronouns, and adjectives that people fall into preassigned roles. Because gender-biased language fails to reflect the diversity of contemporary society, it is inaccurate. Replace nouns that imply gender exclusivity—for example, *chairman* or *spokesman*—with gender-neutral alternatives—for example, *chairperson* or *spokesperson*.

Avoid using gender-specific pronouns when their antecedents are not gender specific. The most common concern is the generic use of a masculine pronoun (*he, him, his, himself*), as in this sentence: "A psychiatrist is bound by professional oath to keep his patients' records confidential." Although this usage was once acceptable, today's writers and readers expect pronoun use to be inclusive, not exclusionary. Solutions include using alternative pronouns ("A psychiatrist is bound by professional oath to keep his or her patients' records confidential."), plural forms ("Psychiatrists are bound by professional oath to keep their patients' records confidential."), and omission of the pronoun when no confusion is likely ("A psychiatrist is bound by professional oath to keep patients' records confidential.").

Avoid using gender-related adjectives when other modifiers create similar meaning without bias or when gender is not an issue. "The male nurse was both competent and friendly, reassuring the patient and family members" is better presented this way: "The nurse was both competent and friendly, reassuring the patient and family members."

Other Forms of Bias

Be sensitive to the ways in which your language characterizes people by age, class, religion, region, physical and mental ability, or sexual orientation. Do your word choices create stereotypical impressions that disrupt your discussions? Do they convey unintended but negative feelings? Will they offend potential readers and therefore distract them from your ideas? Examine your writing carefully for instances of these kinds of bias and explore alternative ways to convey your meaning.

Biased Language in a Historical Context

Historical texts often contain language that violates today's standards of usage. However, if you quote from such a text, you should retain the original language. The date in the in-text reference will allow readers to place the language in the correct historical context. If the language is particularly troublesome, you may insert an asterisk (*) following the first use of the word or phrase and provide commentary in a footnote.

Preparing the Reference List and In-Text Citations

The reference list provides comprehensive information on each of the sources used in a paper. By listing the author (or authors) of each source—along with publication dates, full titles, and information about publishers (producers, distributors, or websites)—writers ensure that readers can locate sources for further study.

Sources that appear in the reference list must be cited in the paper using parallel information. For example, if a reference-list entry includes two authors, then the in-text citation must also include both authors' names (see "In-Text Citations" later in this chapter). For this reason, writers should prepare reference-list entries for sources before writing the paper.

This chapter includes detailed discussions of the information required for a reference list, as well as its formatting require-ments; Chapters 5 through 8 provide explanations and examples of the most commonly used sources for APA papers. In addi-tion, this book provides information on some sources that are not traditionally used in APA journal articles (the writing done by professionals) but that are potentially useful for students' writing; the principles of APA documentation style have been applied in preparing these sample entries.

4a   The Reference List—An Overview

A reference list is an alphabetically arranged listing of sources used in a paper. It starts on a new page immediately after the last text page of the paper, continues the page numbering, and is also double-spaced. It is introduced by the word *References* (centered but not italicized); if the reference list continues on subsequent pages, no additional heading is required for those pages. Entries in the reference list follow the formats described in this chapter. (See pages 119 and 130 for the reference lists of the sample papers.)

4b   Information for APA Entries

Entries for the reference list vary because of the different informa-tion they include. All, however, must follow an established order for presenting information.

1. **Authors (and editors).** Take names from the first page of an article or from the title page of a book. Search online sources carefully because authors' names are not always placed in the most logical locations. Authors' or editors' names are listed in the order in which they appear (not alphabetical order), and initials are used instead of first or middle names. *All* authors' names are inverted (last name first), not just the name of the first author. In some circumstances, groups, corporations, institutions, or organizations publish works under their collective names, rather than those of individual authors; in such cases, the names are spelled out completely. If an article or book has eight or more authors, the first six are listed, followed by ellipsis points (three spaced periods) and the name of the last author. Note: When a source has no author, the entry begins with the title, followed by the date.

2. **Publication dates.** For articles in scholarly journals and books, include the publication year in parentheses. For sources that use specific dates—such as popular magazines, newspapers, television broadcasts, or websites—include the year and the month or the year, month, and day in parentheses.

3. **Titles.** List titles completely, taking information from the first page of an article or from the title page of a book. Include both titles and subtitles, no matter how long they are.

4. **Additional information.** Include any of the following information in the order presented here if it is listed on the first page of the article, essay, chapter or other subsection, or the title page of the book:
   • Translator
   • Edition number
   • Volume number
   • Issue number (if the journal is paginated separately by issue)
   • Inclusive pages

5. **Facts of publication.** For periodicals, take the volume number, issue number (if needed), and date from the first few pages in journals and magazines, often in combination with the table of contents, or from the masthead (a listing of information at the top of the first page of newspapers). For books, use the first city listed on the title page and provide a two-letter abbreviation for the state or the full name of the foreign country. Take the publisher's name from the

title page, presenting it in abbreviated form (see the following box for explanations of how to shorten publishers' names and Chapters 5 through 8 for samples within entries). Use the most recent date from the copyright page (which immediately follows the title page).

6. **Retrieval information.** For electronic sources, provide a retrieval statement, a phrase or sentence that explains how to access the source, to direct readers to the electronic copy. (See page 103 for alternative patterns for presenting retrieval statements.)

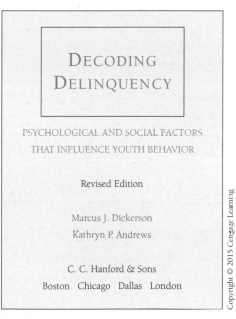

DECODING
DELINQUENCY

PSYCHOLOGICAL AND SOCIAL FACTORS
THAT INFLUENCE YOUTH BEHAVIOR

Revised Edition

Marcus J. Dickerson
Kathryn P. Andrews

C. C. Hanford & Sons
Boston Chicago Dallas London

Copyright © 2015 Cengage Learning

Sample title page

- Authors (last names and initials; in the order on the title page)
- Date (the most recent one)
- Title (including the subtitle)
- Edition (in abbreviated form)
- City (the first one listed) and state
- Publisher (in shortened form)

Dickerson, M. J., & Andrews, K. P. (2012). *Decoding delinquency: Psychological and social factors that influence youth behavior* **(Rev. ed.). Boston, MA: Hanford.**

C. C. HANFORD & SONS
Boston   Chicago   Dallas   London

C. C. Hanford & Sons

214 Channel Street, Boston, MA 02211, USA

Published in the United States by C. C. Hanford & Sons, Boston

www.cchanford.com

Information on this title: www.cchanford.com/94284301

© 2009, 2012 C. C. Hanford & Sons

ALL RIGHTS RESERVED. No part of this work covered by the copyright herein may be reproduced, transmitted, stored, or used in any form or by any means graphic, electronic, or mechanical, including but not limited to photocopying, recording, scanning, digitizing, taping, Web distribution, information networks, or information storage and retrieval systems, except as permitted under Section 107 or 108 of the 1976 United States Copyright Act, without the prior permission of the publisher.

First printed 2009
Reprinted 2010 (twice)

Printed in the United States

ISBN-13: 121-0-443-91263-6
ISBN-10: 0-443-91263-6

C. C. Hanford & Sons has no responsibility for the persistence or accuracy of URLs for external or third-party Internet websites referred to in this book, and does not guarantee that any content on such websites is, or will remain, accurate or appropriate.

Sample copyright page

4c   Format for APA Entries

To ensure easy reading, entries for the reference list must follow this format.

• **Indentation patterns.** Begin the first line of each entry at the left margin; indent subsequent lines five to seven spaces (½ inch), using the "Indent" feature.

- **Authors' names.** Because entries must be arranged in alphabetical order, invert all authors' names (Haley, R.) and use an ampersand (&), not the word *and,* to join the names of multiple authors (Haley, R., & Taylor, J.).

- **Authorless sources.** When no author is identified, list the source by title. Alphabetize a reference-list entry by using the primary words of the title (excluding *a, an,* or *the*). When an authorless book has an editor, you can, as an alternative, begin the entry with his or her last name and first and middle initials (with the abbreviation *Ed.* in parentheses but not italicized), followed by a period.

- **Article titles.** Include full titles, using sentence-style capitalization. Article titles are not enclosed in quotation marks in a reference-list entry, although they are placed in quotation marks and use headline-style capitalization in in-text citations and in the paper.

- **Periodical titles.** Present the titles of periodicals in headline style (all major words capitalized). Follow the title with a comma and the volume number. Italicize the title *and* the volume number, including the separating comma and the comma that follows the volume number.

- **Issue numbers.** If a journal paginates issues separately, place the issue number in parentheses after the volume number; no space separates the volume number from the issue number, and the parentheses and issue number are *not* italicized. Both volume and issue numbers are presented as Arabic, not Roman, numerals.

- **Titles of books.** Present the titles of books with sentence-style capitalization. The title is italicized. (Headline-style capitalization is used in the paper.)

- **Publishers' names.** Shorten the names of commercial publishers to a brief but clear form, using only the main elements of their names (Cengage, not Cengage Learning) and dropping descriptive titles (Publishers, Company, Incorporated). However, use the complete names of organizations and corporations that serve as publishers and university presses, retaining the words *Books* and *Press* whenever they are part of a publisher's name. If a work has co-publishers, include both publishers' names, separated by a hyphen or an en dash (Harvard–Belknap Press).

- **Punctuation within entries.** Separate major sections of entries (author, date, title, and publication information) with periods, including elements enclosed in parentheses or brackets; the period used with the abbreviation of an

Shortened Forms of Publishers' Names

Use the full names of associations and corporations that serve as publishers.	American Psychological Association, National Council of Teachers of English (These publishers' names appear in their full forms.)
Use the full names of university presses.	Harvard University Press, University of Illinois Press (These publishers' names appear in their full forms.)
Use full names for government publishers.	U.S. Government Printing Office (This name appears in its full form.)
Drop given names or initials.	Harry N. Abrams is shortened to Abrams.
Use the first of multiple names.	Farrar, Straus, and Giroux is shortened to Farrar.
Drop corporation designations: *Publishers, Company, Incorporated,* and so on.	Doubleday and Co., Inc. is shortened to Doubleday.
Retain the words *Books* and *Press.*	Bantam Books, American Psychiatric Press (These publishers' names appear in their full forms.)

author's first or middle name substitutes for this period. However, separate the place of publication from the publisher's name with a colon. When an entry ends with a DOI or URL, no period is required to close the entry.

- **Spacing within entries.** One space separates elements in APA entries. However, when a journal paginates issues separately, the issue number (in parentheses) follows the volume number without a space.

- **Abbreviations.** Use abbreviations for standard parts of periodicals, books, and other print materials. (See the following box for a list of acceptable abbreviations.)

- **Page numbers.** When citing articles in periodicals or chapters or other portions of complete works, list numbers completely (pp. 176–179, not pp. 176–9 or pp. 176–79), separated by a hyphen or an en dash. Journals and magazines list page numbers without page abbreviations; however, page references for newspapers, books, and other print materials use the abbreviations *p.* (for page) and *pp.* (for pages), not italicized. No commas are used to separate digits of numbers one thousand or larger when citing pages (pp. 1295–1298). When articles appear on non-consecutive pages, list all pages, separated by commas (pp. 34–35, 38, 54–55, 57, 59).
- **Line spacing.** The entire reference list is double-spaced.

Acceptable Abbreviations

Digital object identifier	DOI or doi
edition	ed.
Editor (Editors)	Ed. (Eds.)
no date	n.d.
No place of publication	N.p.
no publisher	n.p.
Number	No.
page (pages)	p. (pp.)
Part	Pt.
Revised edition	Rev. ed.
Second edition, fifth edition	2nd ed., 5th ed. (superscript is not used)
Supplement	Suppl.
Technical report	Tech. Rep.
Translator	Trans.
Uniform resource locator	URL
Volume (Volumes)	Vol. (Vols.)

4d   Alphabetizing the Reference List

The reference list must be in alphabetical order, which seems simple enough. Reality often proves more complicated, however, so use the guidelines in the following box.

Alphabetizing the Reference List

CIRCUMSTANCES	RULE AND SAMPLE
Letter-by-letter style	Alphabetize one letter at a time: *Baker, R. L.* precedes *Baker, W. S.; Our American Heritage* comes before *Our American Legacy*.
"Nothing precedes something"	The space that follows a name supersedes the letters that follow: *Wood, T. S.,* precedes *Woodman, K. F.*
Prefixes	Prefixes are alphabetized as they appear, not as if they appeared in full form: *MacDonald, J. B.,* precedes *McDonald, B. V.*
Names with prepositions	Names that incorporate prepositions are alphabetized as if they were spelled closed: *De Forest, A. M.,* precedes *Denton, R. L.* (Consult a dictionary regarding patterns for names in different languages.)
Multiple works by the same author	Arrange selections in chronological order: *Sparks, C. G.* (2008) precedes *Sparks, C. G.* (2009)
Single-author and multiple-author works	Single-author works precede multiple-author works: *Kelly, M. J.,* precedes *Kelly, M. J., & Davidson, P. G.*
Groups, institutions, or organizations as authors	Alphabetize group, institutional, or organizational authors by major words in their completely spelled-out names (omitting *a, an,* or *the*): *American Psychological Association* precedes *Anderson, V. W.*
Authorless works	Authorless works are alphabetized by the first significant words in their titles (omitting *a, an,* or *the*): *The price of poverty* precedes *Stewart, R. P.*
Numerals in titles	Numerals in titles are alphabetized as if they were spelled out: "The 10 common errors of research" precedes *Twelve angry men.*

4e   In-Text Citations

APA documentation has two areas of emphasis: (a) the authors of source materials and (b) the year in which sources were published or presented. This pattern is commonly referred to as the author–date style.

When incorporating information from a source, provide an in-text citation that includes, at minimum, the author's last name and the year of publication or presentation. The complexity of some sources may require the inclusion of additional information.

Patterns for In-Text Citations

An in-text citation (also called a parenthetical note) corresponds to an entry in the reference list at the end of the paper. The information in an entry for the reference list determines what information appears in a citation in the text. For example, if a reference-list entry for a source begins with the author's name, then the author's name appears in the in text citation. If a reference-list citation for a source begins with the title, however, then the title (or a shortened version of it) appears in the in-text citation. If these correlations are clear and consistent, readers can turn from the paper's in-text citation to the reference list and easily locate the full entry for the source.

Basic Forms of In-Text Citations

To avoid disrupting the text, in-text citations identify only the last name of the author (or authors) or a brief version of the title under which the source appears in the reference list, followed by the year of publication (even when reference-list entries require the month or month and day). For the sake of clarity and smoothness, you may incorporate some of the necessary information in your sentences. After the author and date have been introduced, the date may be omitted in subsequent references within the same paragraph.

Educational bodies—accrediting agencies, boards of education, and school boards—must acknowledge that assessment of teaching performance may focus on different issues: "Evaluating whether teachers promote student learning is one thing, while evaluating whether they raise student test scores is another" (Papay, 2012, pp. 131–132). Unless they do

Shortened Forms of Titles

- **Use initial words of the title.** Because readers will use the short title to find the full title in the reference list, use words at the beginning. "When Teachers Don't Make the Grade" can logically be shortened to "When Teachers."

- **Omit articles.** *A, an,* and *the* should be dropped from the shortened title. *A Long Day's Journey into Night* can be shortened to *Long Day's Journey.*

- **Omit subtitles.** Omit the clarifying information in the second part of a two-part title. "Paycare: The High Cost of Insurance-based Medicine" can be shortened to "Paycare."

- **Omit prepositional phrases.** Omit prepositional phrases at the ends of titles. *The Price of Poverty* can be shortened to *Price.*

- **Make the short title brief but readable.** Remember that the short title will be part of your text and should, consequently, read well. *The Chicago Manual of Style* shortens to *Chicago Manual; Chicago* alone might read awkwardly.

- **Retain punctuation patterns.** Follow the punctuation patterns required in the text: titles of articles, chapters, poems, and other brief works are placed in quotation marks; titles of journals, books, films, and other long works are italicized. Punctuate the shortened forms of titles as you would the complete forms. *APA Dictionary of Psychology* could be shortened to *APA Dictionary,* but it remains in italics.

so, assessment will be ineffective, and the results will be potentially damaging.

OR

Educational bodies—accrediting agencies, boards of education, and school boards—must acknowledge that assessment of teaching performance may focus on different issues. Papay (2012) observed that "evaluating whether teachers promote student learning is one thing, while evaluating whether they raise student test scores is another" (pp. 131–132). Unless this difference is noted, assessment will be ineffective, and the results will be potentially damaging.

Reference-list entry

Papay, J. N. (2012). Refocusing the debate: Assessing the purposes
 and tools of teacher evaluation. *Harvard Educational
 Review, 1,* 123–141.

In special cases, the rule of using only the author's last name and
the date is superseded.

Patterns for In-Text Citations

SPECIAL CIRCUMSTANCES	RULE AND SAMPLE
Two authors with the same last name	Include initials with the last name: (Barratt, J. D., 2011), distinct from (Barratt, L. K., 2012).
Multiple works by the same author (same year)	Use letters to distinguish the sources: (Morrison, 2010a), distinct from (Morrison, 2010b). The letters indicate the alphabetical order of the titles.
Multiple works by the same author (same note)	To cite several works by the same author (all included in the reference list), include the author's name and all dates in chronological order, separated by commas. (Vidich, 2009, 2011, 2012).
Three, four, or five authors	The first notation includes all names (Greenly, Hopkins, & Sullivan, 2012). Subsequent citations use the first author's name and et al., not italicized: (Greenly et al., 2012).
Six or more authors	Beginning with the first notation, use only the first author's name and et al., not italicized: (Austen et al., 2010).
Two or more works by different authors (same note)	To cite several works by different authors in the same note, list each author (in alphabetical order) and date, separated by semicolons: (Bennet, 2012; Greene, 2009; Swift, 2010).

continued on next page

SPECIAL CIRCUMSTANCES	RULE AND SAMPLE
Organization as author	In the first note, present the organization's name in full, with an abbreviation in brackets: (American Association of Community Psychiatrists [AACP], 2012). Use the shortened form in subsequent citations: (AACP, 2012).
No author	Include a shortened version of the title, appropriately capitalized and punctuated, and the year: ("Optimum Performance," 2011); (*Common Ground*, 2012). If *Anonymous* is the *explicit* attribution of a work, it is used in the author position, but not italicized: (Anonymous, 2010).
Multiple publication dates	Include both dates, separated by a slash: (Jagger & Richards, 1994/2001).
Reference works	List by author if applicable (Sternberg, 2012) or by a shortened form of the title ("Artificial Intelligence," 2012).
Parts of sources	When citing only a portion of a source—for example, a page to identify a quotation or a chapter in a general reference—include the author or title as appropriate, the date, and clarifying information: (Thomas, 2010, p. 451); (Spindrell, 2009, Chapters 2–3).
Personal communication	Cite e-mail, correspondence, memos, interviews, and so on by listing the person's name, the clarifying phrase *personal communication* (not italicized), and the specific date (L. R. Bates, personal communication, March 7, 2011).

(NOTE: Although cited in the text, personal communications do not have entries in the reference list. Initials are also used with the person's last name.)

4f　Quotations

When an author's manner of expression is unique or when his or her ideas or language are difficult to paraphrase or summarize, quote the passage in your text. To avoid plagiarism, reproduce quoted material word for word, including exact spelling and punctuation, separate the material from your text, and prepare an accurate citation.

The pattern for incorporating a quotation varies depending on its length. In-text citations for quotations also include specific page references.

Brief Quotations (Fewer Than 40 Words)

A quotation of fewer than 40 words appears within a normal paragraph, with the author's words enclosed in quotation marks. The in-text citation, placed in parentheses, follows the closing quotation mark, whether it is in the middle or at the end of a sentence; if the quotation ends the sentence, the sentence's period follows the closing parenthesis. The citation includes the author's name and the publication date (unless these have been previously mentioned in the text), as well as a specific page reference, introduced with the abbreviation *p.* or *pp.* (not italicized). For example:

> The law is inextricably linked to culture and, at times, popular culture. Reacting to controversial films about teenagers in the 1950s, "both civil rights activists and segregationists harnessed popular outrage and fear over delinquent youth" (Walker, 2010, p. 1913). The result was a cultural collision about race, class, and ethnicity.

Reference-list entry

Walker, A. (2010). *Blackboard Jungle*: Delinquency, desegregation, and the cultural politics of *Brown. Columbia Law Review, 110,* 1911–1953.

Long Quotations (40 or More Words)

A quotation of 40 or more words is set off from a normal paragraph in an indented block paragraph. After an introductory statement, start the quotation on a new line, indented five to seven spaces or ½ inch (use the "Indent" feature to maintain the indentation throughout the quotation). Quotation marks do not appear at the opening and closing of a block quotation. Like the surrounding text, the quotation is double-spaced. Note that

Concerns About Quotations

Although quotations can enhance a paper by presenting the ideas of other writers in their own words, the overuse of quotations can become distracting. Therefore, assess the value of quotations by asking the following questions.

- **Style.** Is the style so distinctive that you cannot say the same thing as well or as clearly in your own words?
- **Vocabulary.** Is the vocabulary technical and therefore difficult to translate into your own words?
- **Reputation.** Is the author so well known or so important that the quotation can lend authority to your paper?
- **Points of contention.** Does the author's material raise doubts or questions or make points with which you disagree?

If you answer yes to any of these questions, then using the quotation is appropriate. If not, summarize or paraphrase the material instead.

the period precedes the in-text citation with a block quotation. For example:

Expressing current uncertainty about the causes of allergy patterns, Prescott and Allen (2011) observed:

> Allergic disease has been linked to the modern lifestyle including changing dietary patterns, changing intestinal commensal bacteria and vehicular pollution. It is not yet known whether the rise in food allergy is a harbinger of earlier and more severe effects of these pervasive environmental changes or whether additional or unrelated lifestyle factors are implicated. (p. 155)

In modern societies, which prize both certainty and attributable blame, this kind of inconclusiveness is disturbing.

Reference-list entry

Prescott, S., & Allen, K. J. (2011). Food allergy: Riding the second wave of the allergy epidemic. *Pediatric Allergy and Immunology, 22,* 155–160.

Punctuation With Quotations

Single Quotation Marks

To indicate an author's use of quotation marks within a brief quotation (which is set off by double quotation marks), change the source's punctuation to single quotation marks, as in this example:

In an effort to contextualize and to clarify the current debate about gun laws, Brandl and Stroshine (2010) stated that "the distinction between the 'legal' gun market and the 'illegal' gun market is a fuzzy one, at best. The distinction relates most directly to how the gun was acquired, the characteristics of the person who acquired the gun, and how the gun has been used" (p. 287).

Reference-list entry

Brandl, S. G., & Stroshine, M. S. (2010). The relationship between gun and gun buyer characteristics and firearm time-to-crime. *Criminal Justice Policy Review, 22,* 285–300.

Because long block quotations do not begin and end with quotation marks, the source's quotation marks remain double, as in this example:

Skolnick (2010) noted that police behavior, from one perspective, developed because of work experiences, but also observed.

> An alternative explanation for police behavior suggested that the characteristics, values, and opinions an officer brings with [him or her] to [the] job were better predictors of behavior. Police work attracted certain types of people whose behavior was more a product of their general personality, not any "working personality" formed on the job. (p. 10)

Until additional studies are completed, this "nature versus nurture" debate will continue.

Reference-list entry

Skolnick, J. (2010). Police personality: Are police officers different from the rest of us? In A. B. Thistlethwaite & J. D. Wooldredge (Eds.), *Forty studies that changed criminal justice: Explorations into the history of criminal justice research* (pp. 6–13). Upper Saddle River, NJ: Pearson–Prentice Hall.

Brackets

Use brackets to indicate that you have either added words for clarity or introduced a substitution within a quotation. Most often, the words you add will be specific nouns to substitute for pronouns that are vague outside the context of the original work. However, you may substitute a different tense of the same verb (for example, *used* for *use*). *NOTE:* A change in the capitalization at the beginning of a sentence, as well as a change in end punctuation to fit your syntax, does not require the use of brackets.

In assessing issues of America's increasing obesity, Oliver (2006) observed that the "BMI [Body-Mass Index] remains the basis for much of our official health policy today, both in the way we think of obesity and how we measure it" (p. 20). However, weight, by itself, is not the only predictor of health.

The complete form of the abbreviation provides clarity for readers.

Reference-list entry

Oliver, J. E. (2006). *Fat politics: The real story behind America's obesity epidemic*. New York, NY: Oxford University Press.

NOTE: Do not change dated language or material to make it more acceptable by today's standards; rather, let the material stand on its own and provide your own separate commentary. (See page 58.)

Ellipsis Points

Use ellipsis points—three spaced periods—to indicate where words have been omitted within a quotation. Ellipsis points are unnecessary at the beginning or end of a quotation, unless a quotation begins or ends in the middle of a sentence. To indicate an omission between sentences, retain the preceding sentence's punctuation (producing four spaced periods).

Epstein (2012) explained the challenge of learning for the elderly in this way:

> ... as we age, the degradation of sensory and working memory systems makes it increasingly difficult for us to transfer information into long-term storage. That's why, if you are over 50, you are more likely to remember the lyrics to a Beatles song than to any song you have heard in the past 20 years.... Our ability to learn new things is extraordinary when we are young and peaks in our teens. We can learn after that, but it becomes increasingly difficult. (pp. 50, 76)

This, in part, accounts for the difficulties that the elderly have in learning to use new technologies and dealing with new processes.

[First omission: *But*. Second omission: "To put this another way . . ."]

Reference-list entry

Epstein, R. (2012, October). Brutal truths: About aging and the brain. *Discover, 33,* 48–50, 76.

5   Citing Periodicals

Most often affiliated with professional organizations, journals are scholarly publications whose articles are subjected to careful review. Often called refereed journals, they are the mainstay of much research because they present ideas and information developed by scholars and specialists—and reviewed by scholars—for an audience of scholars. Magazines, in contrast, are commercial publications that present ideas and information for general readers who are nonspecialists; they provide nontechnical discussions and general reactions to issues. Newspapers, published daily or weekly, provide nearly instantaneous reactions to issues in primary stories and more reflective discussions in editorials and feature articles. These periodicals provide reports on research and discussions of contemporary ideas and issues of importance to writers of researched papers.

To cite periodicals in a reference list, follow the guidelines given in this chapter.

5a   An Article in a Journal With Continuous Paging

A journal with continuous paging numbers the pages of a volume consecutively, even though each issue of the journal has a separate number. For example, *Journal of Research in Crime and Delinquency* volume 48 (representing 2011) has numbered issues that are continuously paginated: issue number 1 (February) includes pages 1–142, number 2 (May) spans pages 143–324, number 3 (August) continues with pages 325–506, and so on.

When an article comes from a journal with continuous paging, list its author first, followed by the year of publication and the title of the article with sentence-style capitalization (without quotation marks). Next, include the title of the journal (with headline-style capitalization), a comma, the volume number, and another comma (all italicized). Finish the entry by listing the inclusive page numbers, without a page abbreviation.

Harrison, R. L., & Westwood, M. J. (2009). Preventing vicarious traumatization of mental health therapists: Identifying protective practices. *Psychotherapy: Theory, Research, Practice, Training, 46,* 203–219.

> **In-text citation** (Harrison & Westwood, 2009)

Kinports, K. (2011). The Supreme Court's love-hate relationship with Miranda. *Journal of Criminal Law and Criminology, 101,* 375–440.

> **In-text citation** (Kinports, 2011)

5b An Article in a Journal With Separate Paging

Although few current journals page their issues separately, some older journals may follow this pattern. A journal with separate paging begins each numbered issue with page 1, even though a group of issues is assigned a single volume number. For example, until recently, *Women and Health* numbered issues separately: Volume 44 (representing 2006–2007) began each issue on a new page: issue number 1 (2006) included pages 1–136, issue number 2 (2007) spanned pages 1–134, issue number 3 (2007) covered pages 1–122, and so on.

When a journal has separate paging for each issue, follow the volume number with the issue number, in parentheses; no space separates the volume from the issue, and the issue number and its parentheses are not italicized. All other information in the entry is the same as that of an entry for a journal with continuous paging.

McDonald, T. P., Poertner, J., & Jennings, M. A. (2007). Permanency for children in foster care: A competing risks analysis. *The Journal of Social Science Research, 33*(4), 45–56.

> **First in-text citation** (McDonald, Poertner, & Jennings, 2007)
>
> **Subsequent citations** (McDonald et al., 2007)

Woods, D., & Polizzi, D. (2008). Shoot me! An overview of suicide-by-cop. *Law Enforcement Executive Forum, 8*(2), 49–60.

> **In-text citation** (Woods & Polizzi, 2008)

5c   An Abstract

Although writers most often refer to entire articles, in very special circumstances (for example, when an abstract's summary of key principles is succinct or quotable), you may want to cite only the abstract. In those rare instances, first prepare a full citation of the article; however, insert the word *Abstract,* not italicized, within brackets after the article's title. The period that normally follows the title follows the closing bracket.

McBride, M. E., Waldrop, W. B., Fehr, J. J., Boulet, J. R., & Murray, D. J. (2011). Simulation in pediatrics: The reliability and validity of a multiscenario assessment [Abstract]. *Pediatrics, 128,* 335–343.

> **First in-text citation** (McBride, Waldrop, Fehr, Boulet, & Murray, 2011)
>
> **Subsequent citations** (McBride et al., 2011)

Shermer, L. O., Rose, K. C., & Hoffman, A. (2011). Perceptions and credibility: Understanding the nuances of eyewitness testimony [Abstract]. *Journal of Contemporary Justice, 27,* 183–203.

> **First in-text citation** (Shermer, Rose, & Hoffman, 2011)
>
> **Subsequent citations** (Shermer et al., 2011)

5d   An Article in a Monthly Magazine

An article from a monthly magazine is listed by author. The date is given by year and month, separated by a comma, in parentheses. The article title appears next with sentence-style capitalization. The title of the magazine, with headline-style capitalization, is followed by a comma, the volume number, and the issue number (if there is one); all but the issue number and the parentheses that enclose it are italicized. The entry ends with inclusive page numbers listed without a page abbreviation. Note that only the year is included in the in-text citation, not the year and month.

Gorman, C. (2010, October). Closing the health gap. *Scientific American, 303*(4), 34, 36.

> **In-text citation** (Gorman, 2010)

Madu, C. (2010, March–April). A cure for crime. *Psychology Today, 43*(2), 12.

> **In-text citation** (Madu, 2010)

5e   An Article in a Weekly Magazine

The entry for a weekly magazine is identical to the entry for a monthly magazine except that the date of publication (along with the year and month) is included in parentheses. In the corresponding in-text citation, however, only the year is required.

Begley, S. (2010, February 8). The depressing news about
    antidepressants. *Newsweek, 155*(6), 34–41.

> **In-text citation** (Begley, 2010)

Gibbs, N. (2011, March 21). Zero tolerance, zero sense.
    Time, 177(11), 62.

> **In-text citation** (Gibbs, 2011)

5f   An Article in a Newspaper

An entry for a newspaper article resembles that for a magazine, except that section numbers or letters are included, and paging is indicated with a page abbreviation (*p.* or *pp.*, not italicized).

When sections are indicated by letters, they are presented along with the page numbers, without intervening punctuation or space. However, when newspaper sections are numbered, a colon separates the section from the page number.

Pogrebin, R. (2010, April 22). A mother's loss, a daughter's story.
    The New York Times, pp. E1, E9.

> **In-text citation** (Pogrebin, 2010)

Notice that this article appears on nonconsecutive pages.

Sharma, A., Anand, G., Bahree, M., & Pokharel, K. (2011, July 3).
    The ailing health of a growing nation. *The Wall Street Journal,*
    pp. A1, A10.

> **First in-text citation** (Sharma, Anand, Bahree, & Pokharel, 2011)
> **Subsequent citations** (Sharma et al., 2011)

5g   An Article in a Newsletter

The entry for an article in a newsletter follows the pattern for a magazine: It includes the author, date, title of selection, title of newsletter, volume number, issue number, and inclusive pages (without page abbreviations). If a newsletter appears seasonally, include such identifying information along with the year (2012, Spring).

H1N1 pandemic vaccine safety: Results from clinical trials. (2010).
    Immunization Newsletter, 32(2), 5.

> **In-text citation** ("H1N1," 2010)

Kemp, P. M., Winecker, R. E., & Langman, L. J. (2011, July).
    A world of knowledge in forensic toxicology.
    Academic News, 41(4), 7, 34.

    First in-text citation (Kemp, Winecker, & Langman, 2011)

    Subsequent citations (Kemp et al., 2011)

When pages are not sequential, list them all, separated by commas.

5h   An Editorial

The entry for an editorial—an opinion-based essay—resembles that for a magazine or newspaper article, with one exception: The word *Editorial* (not italicized) is placed within brackets immediately after the title of the essay, if there is one. The period that normally follows the title follows the closing bracket.

Cohen, R. (2012, December 7). Thanks for not sharing [Editorial].
    The New York Times, p. 1.

    In-text citation (Cohen, 2012)

Goti, J. M. (2010). A turbulent past and the problem of memory
    [Editorial]. *International Journal of Transitional Justice, 4,*
    153–165.

    In-text citation (Goti, 2010)

5i   A Letter to the Editor

Following the author's name and the publication date, include the phrase *Letter to the editor* (not italicized) in brackets, followed by a period. The rest of the entry follows the pattern appropriate for the periodical.

Kunisaki, C. (2011). [Letter to the editor]. *Journal of Surgical
    Oncology, 104,* 333.

    In-text citation (Kunisaki, 2011)

Large, M., & Ryan, C. J. (2012). Screening for suicide: A comment
    on Steeg et al. [Letter to the editor]. *Psychological Medicine,
    42*(9), 2011-2012.

    In-text citation (Large & Ryan, 2012)

Notice that this letter to the editor has an attributed title.

5j   A Review

After the author, date, and review title (if there is one), include a descriptive phrase that begins "Review of the book (motion picture, music recording, car, computer game)" and ends with the specific product name; enclose this information in brackets, followed by a period. Then continue the entry as is appropriate for the source.

Earl, J. (2011). [Review of the book *Crimes of dissent: Civil disobedience, criminal justice, and the politics of conscience*, by J. S. Lovell]. *Law and Society, 45*, 224–225.

In-text citation (Earl, 2011)

Rosen, D. (2012). [Review of the book *Improving medical outcomes: The psychology of doctor-patient visits*, by J. Leavitt & F. Leavitt]. *Journal of the American Medical Association, 307*, 514.

In-text citation (Rosen, 2012)

5k   A Secondary Source

The authors of primary sources report their own research and ideas; the authors of secondary sources report the research and ideas of others. For example, in an article titled "Rationale and Evidence for Menu-Labeling Legislation" (*American Journal of Preventative Medicine*), Roberto, Schwartz, and Brownell (2009) reported on a study showing that federally mandated menu labeling at fast-food restaurants did, in fact, influence consumers to select foods with fewer calories; this article is considered a primary source. Yang and Nichols (2011) incorporated information and assessments from Roberto, Schwartz, and Brownell's original article in their article "Obesity and Health System Reform: Private vs. Public Responsibility"; Yang and Nichols's article is a secondary source. Although it is best to use the original or primary source (Roberto, Schwartz, & Brownell, 2009), sometimes you must use the secondary source (Yang & Nichols, 2011).

Yang, Y. T., & Nichols, L. M. (2011). Obesity and health system reform: Private vs. public responsibility. *Journal of Law, Medicine, and Ethics, 39*, 380–386.

In-text commentary and citation
Roberto, Schwartz, and Brownell (2009) observed that when menu labels are prominently displayed, customers will, with some regularity, select food with fewer calories (as cited in Yang & Nichols, 2011).

6 Citing Books and Other Separately Published Materials

Reference-List Entries for Books and Other Separately Published Materials

Books provide comprehensive, extended discussions of topics. Those published by scholarly or university presses are often targeted to specialists in particular fields and provide a broad range of technical information and complex analyses. Those published by trade (commercial) publishers are often directed to nonspecialists.

Because books take several years to produce, they frequently provide reflective interpretations that have the benefit of critical distance. Consequently, they provide balance in research.

To cite books in a reference list, follow the guidelines in this chapter.

6a A Book by One Author

The entry for a book by a single author begins with his or her name, followed by the year in parentheses, the title, the city and state (or country) of publication, and the publisher. A book title is presented in italics, with sentence-style capitalization.

Dickey, C. (2009). *Securing the city: Inside America's best counterterror force—the NYPD*. New York, NY: Simon.

> **In-text citation** (Dickey, 2009)

Weiner, M. F. (2010). *Power, protest, and the public school: Jewish and African American struggles in New York City.*
New Brunswick, NJ: Rutgers University Press.

> **In-text citation** (Weiner, 2010)

6b A Book by Two or More Authors

When a book has multiple authors, their names appear in the order presented on the title page, not alphabetical order. The names of two to seven authors are listed, with all of their names inverted. An ampersand (&) joins the last two names. If a book has eight or more authors, the first six are listed, followed by ellipsis points (three spaced periods) and the name of the last author.

Lazarus, R. S., & Lazarus, B. N. (2006). *Coping with aging.*
New York, NY: Oxford University Press.

> **In-text citation** (Lazarus & Lazarus, 2006)

Wright, J. P., Tibbetts, S. G., & Daigle, L. E. (2008). *Criminals in the making: Criminality across the life course*. Thousand Oaks, CA: Sage.

> **First in-text citation** (Wright, Tibbetts, & Daigle, 2008)
>
> **Subsequent citations** (Wright et al., 2008)

6c A Book With No Author Named

When no author or editor is named, list the book by title. When an editor is listed, begin with the editor's name. The following source is listed by title.

Federal regulatory directory: The essential guide to the history,
    organization, and impact of U.S. federal regulation (15th ed.).
    (2011). Washington, DC: CQ Press–S.

   In-text citation (*Federal Regulatory Directory*, 2011)

The edition number follows the title, in parentheses; notice that
the edition number is not italicized, that the abbreviation for
edition—ed.—is followed by a period, and that another period
follows the closing parenthesis. With an authorless book, the
year follows the title or edition number. (See 6e for the common
pattern of presenting editions.)

   The following source is listed by editor.

VandenBos, G. R. (Ed.). (2007). *APA dictionary of psychology.*
    Washington, DC: American Psychological Association.

   In-text citation (VandenBos, 2007)

6d   A Book With an Organization as Author

When an organization is listed as the author, spell out the name
completely in the author position. When the organization is also
the publisher, use the word *Author,* not italicized, in the publisher
position.

American Psychological Association. (2009). *Publication manual of
    the American Psychological Association* (6th ed.). Washington,
    DC: Author.

   First in-text citation (American Psychological Association
   [APA], 2009)

   Subsequent citations (APA, 2009)

The first in-text citation with an organization as an author includes
the full name, followed by the abbreviated name within brackets;
additional references include only the abbreviated name.

American Hospital Association. (2011). *AHA guide to the health care
    field.* Chicago, IL: Health Forum.

   First in-text citation (American Hospital Association
   [AHA], 2011)

   Subsequent citations (AHA, 2011)

6e   An Edition Other Than the First

The edition number, which appears on the title page, follows the
title of the book, in parentheses. Note that it is not italicized and
that the period that normally follows the title follows the closing
parenthesis instead.

Moritsugu, J., Wong, F. Y., & Duffy, K. G. (2010). *Community psychology* (4th ed.). Boston, MA: Allyn.

> ***First in-text citation*** (Moritsugu, Wong, & Duffy, 2010)

> ***Subsequent citations*** (Moritsugu et al., 2010)

Long, L. L., & Young, M. E. (2007). *Counseling and therapy for couples* (2nd ed.). Belmont, CA: Brooks/Cole–Cengage.

> ***In-text citation*** (Long & Young, 2007)

Note that dual publishers are both listed, separated by an en dash or a hyphen.

6f An Edited Collection

Present an entire edited collection like a traditional book, with the editor's name in the author position.

Foreman, M. D., Milisen, K., & Fulner, T. T. (Eds.). (2010). *Critical care nursing of older adults: Best practices.* New York, NY: Springer.

> ***First in-text citation*** (Foreman, Milisen, & Fulner, 2010)

> ***Subsequent citations*** (Foreman et al., 2010)

Gilde, C. (Ed.). (2007). *Higher education: Open for business.* Lanham, MD: Lexington Books.

> ***In-text citation*** (Gilde, 2007)

6g An Original Selection in an Edited Collection

To cite an original selection in an edited collection, begin with the name of the author of the selection, followed by the date in parentheses and the selection's title (with sentence-style capitalization and no quotation marks). Introduced by the word *In* (not italicized), the collection editor is listed next (his or her name is in normal order, followed by the abbreviation *Ed.* in parentheses, not italicized), followed by a comma. The title of the collection, italicized, is followed by the inclusive page numbers for the selection, with the abbreviation for pages, listed in parentheses. The entry ends with the facts of publication.

Estrin, M., & Malm, C. (2010). State weakness and infectious diseases. In S. E. Rice, C. Graff, & C. Pascul (Eds.), *Confronting poverty: Weak states and U.S. national security* (pp. 167–201). Washington, DC: Brookings Institution Press.

> ***In-text citation*** (Estrin & Malm, 2010)

Lurigio, A. J., & Snowden, J. (2008). Prison culture and the treatment and control of mentally ill offenders. In J. M. Bryne, D. Hummer, & F. S. Taxman (Eds.), *The culture of prison violence* (pp. 164–179). Boston, MA: Prentice Hall.

   In-text citation (Lurigio & Snowden, 2008)

6h A Previously Published Selection in an Edited Collection

When a selection has been reprinted from a work published earlier, provide identifying information in parentheses at the end of the entry. Include the information for the original source, but notice that page numbers appear with the abbreviation for pages (even when the original source is a periodical), and the year follows the page numbers. Also note that the closing parenthesis is not followed by a period.

Bazemore, G., & Day, S. E. (2005). Restoring the balance. Juvenile and community justice. In D. L. Parry (Ed.), *Essential readings in juvenile justice* (pp. 405–414). Upper Saddle River, NJ: Prentice Hall. (Reprinted from *Juvenile Justice, 3*(1), pp. 3–14, 1996)

   In-text citation (Bazemore & Day, 2005)

Soames, S. (2009). The necessary argument. In *Philosophical essays: Vol. 1. Natural language: What it means and how we use it* (pp. 202–207). Princeton, NJ: Princeton University Press. (Reprinted from *Linguistics and Philosophy 14*, pp. 575–580, 1991)

   In-text citation (Soames, 2009)

This reprinted essay appears in the first volume of a multivolume work (see 6k).

6i A Revised or Enlarged Edition

Enclose the description of a revised or enlarged edition in parentheses following the title. As with other editions, the parenthetical information precedes the period that follows the title. This information is not italicized.

Houck, M. M., & Siegel, J. A. (2010). *Fundamentals of forensic science* (Rev. ed.). Burlington, MA: Academic Press.

   In-text citation (Houck & Siegel, 2010)

Jacobs, L. R., & Skocpol, T. (2012). *Health care reform and American politics: What everyone needs to know* (Rev. ed.). New York, NY: Oxford University Press.

   In-text citation (Jacobs & Skocpol, 2012)

6j A Reprinted Book

The entry for a reprinted book begins with the full entry of the version you have used; the entry ends with a parenthetical description of the original publication date, with no period after the closing parenthesis. Note that the in-text citation includes both dates, presented in chronological order, separated by a slash.

Kimmel, A. J. (2007). *Ethical issues in behavioral research: Basic and applied perspectives.* Malden, MA: Wiley-Blackwell. (Original work published 1966)

> **In-text citation** (Kimmel, 1966/2007)

Pritchard, E. W. (2009). *A complete report of the trial of Dr. E. W. Pritchard, for the alleged poisoning of his wife and mother-in-law.* Memphis, TN: General Books. (Original work published 1865)

> **In-text citation** (Pritchard, 1865/2009)

6k A Multivolume Work

When citing a complete multivolume work, the number of volumes appears in parentheses following the title but before the period; if an edition number is required, it precedes the volume number.

Fisher, B. S., & Lab, S. P. (Eds.). (2010). *Encyclopedia of victimology and crime prevention* (Vols. 1–2). Thousand Oaks, CA: Sage Publications.

> **In-text citation** (Fisher & Lab, 2010)

When citing a separately titled volume of a multivolume work, list the multivolume title first, followed by a colon and one space. Then list the separate volume number, followed by a period, and the single volume title. The multivolume title, volume information, and specific title are all italicized. Note that the names of series editors precede those of volume editors; the order of presentation, then, corresponds to the order of the titles.

Boon, K. E., Huq, A., & Lovelace, D. C. (Vol. Eds). (2011). *Terrorism: Commentary on security documents: Vol. 116. Assessing President Obama's national security strategy.* New York, NY: Oxford University Press.

> **First in-text citation** (Boon, Huq, & Lovelace, 2011)
>
> **Subsequent citations** (Boon et al., 2011)

6l An Article in an Encyclopedia or Other Reference Work

To cite an article in an encyclopedia or other reference work, begin with the author's name, when it is available, followed by the date in parentheses. Next list the subject heading under which the material appears (exactly as it appears in the source), without special punctuation. Follow it with the title of the reference work. In parentheses, but before the period that follows the title, include the volume number, if applicable, and the inclusive pages. End the entry with the city and state (or country) of publication and the publisher.

When a reference work has a large editorial board, include the first editor's name and *et al.* (not italicized) to substitute for the other editors' names.

Barber, C. (2009). Gender identity. In E. M. Anderman & L. H. Anderman (Eds.), *Psychology of classroom learning: An encyclopedia* (Vols. 1–2, pp. 428–430). Detroit, MI: Gale–Cengage.

In-text citation (Barber, 2009)

Sulloway, F. J. (2007). Birth order and sibling competition. In R. I. M. Dunbar & L. Barrett (Eds.), *Oxford handbook of evolutionary psychology* (pp. 297–311). New York, NY: Oxford University Press.

In-text citation (Sulloway, 2007)

6m A Work In a Series

If a book is part of a series, that fact is stated on the title page or the facing page. The entry follows the pattern for a similar book, except that the series title (italicized, with headline-style capitalization) appears in a phrase preceding the city of publication and publisher.

Ferguson, A., & Armstrong, E. (2009). *Researching communication disorders*. In *Research and Practices in Applied Linguistics Series*. New York, NY: Palgrave–Macmillan.

In-text citation (Ferguson & Armstrong, 2009)

Lamb, M. E., Hershkowitz, I., Orbach, Y., & Esplin, P. W. (2008). *Tell me what happened: Structured investigative interviews of child victims and witnesses*. In *The Psychology of Crime, Policing, and Law Series*. Hoboken, NJ: Wiley–Blackwell.

First in-text citation (Lamb, Hershkowitz, Orbach, & Esplin, 2008)

Subsequent citations (Lamb et al., 2008)

6n   A Translation

Under most circumstances, the translator of a text is cited in parentheses immediately after the title of the selection (whether it is an essay, chapter, or complete text) but before the closing period for that element.

de Beauvoir, S. (2003). The married woman (H. M. Parshly, Trans.). In S. Hirschberg & T. Hirschberg (Eds.), *Past to present: Ideas that changed our world* (pp. 188–194). Upper Saddle River, NJ: Prentice Hall.

In-text citation (de Beauvoir, 2003)

The previous example indicates that Parshly translated only the selection presented in this entry. Had he translated the entire collection, his name would have appeared after the anthology's title.

Nietzsche, F. (2011). *Beyond good and evil* (H. Zimmern, Trans.). New York, NY: Tribeca Books. (Original work published 1886)

In-text citation (Nietzsche, 1886/2011)

This entry indicates that Zimmern translated the entire book.

6o   A Government Document—Committee, Commission, Department

An entry for a government document follows the pattern used for another similar source. Because many government documents are book-length, that pattern most often applies. Note, however, that APA style requires a publication number for a government document, if available (usually found on the title page or back cover), presented in parentheses after the title; the document number is not italicized. When serving as publisher, the *U.S. Government Printing Office* is spelled out, not abbreviated, and not italicized.

Root, E. D., Allpress, J. L., Cajka, J. C., Lambert, S. B., Savitz, L. A., & Bernard, S. L. (2007). *Emergency preparedness atlas: U.S. nursing home and hospital facilities* (AHRHS 07-0029-2). Rockville, MD: Agency of Healthcare Research and Quality–U.S. Department of Health and Human Services.

In-text citation (Root et al., 2007)

Scaperlanda, M. A. (2009). *Immigration law: A primer*. Washington, DC: Federal Judicial Center.

In-text citation (Scaperlanda, 2009)

6p   A Preface, Introduction, Foreword, Epilogue, or Afterword

When introductory or closing material is titled, it is presented like a selection in a collection; however, a descriptive word (*Preface*,

Epilogue, and so on, not italicized) is enclosed within brackets before the period. Cite pages as they appear in the source, using either lowercase Roman or Arabic numerals.

Untitled material is cited separately by providing a descriptive title (within brackets), followed by complete entry information.

Kassel, J. D., & Veilleux, J. C. (2010). The complex interplay between substance abuse and emotion [Introduction]. In J. D. Kassel (Ed.), *Substance abuse and emotion* (pp. 3–12). Washington, DC: American Psychological Association.

In-text citation (Kassel & Veilleux, 2010)

Nieto, S. (2007). The national mythology and urban teaching [Introduction]. In G. Campano, *Immigrant students and literacy: Reading, writing, and remembering* (pp. 1–6). New York, NY: Teachers College Press.

In-text citation (Nieto, 2007)

6q   A Monograph

To create an entry for a monograph (a separately published, essay-length selection that is sometimes a reprint of a journal article and sometimes an independently prepared selection that is part of a series), include traditional publishing information. However, after the title and in parentheses, include the monograph series title and monograph number, if available; the monograph number is introduced by *No.,* the abbreviation for *number.*

Brown, R., & Stobart, K. (2008). *Understanding boundaries and containment in clinical practice* (Society of Analytical Psychology Monograph). London, England: Karnac.

In-text citation (Brown & Stobart, 2008)

Ginsburg, J., Taylor, T., & Barr, M. S. (2009). *Nurse practitioners in primary care* (A Policy Monograph of the American College of Physicians). Philadelphia, PA: American College of Physicians.

First in-text citation (Ginsburg, Taylor, & Barr, 2009)

Subsequent citations (Ginsburg et al., 2009)

6r   A Pamphlet or Brochure

When a pamphlet or brochure contains clearly presented information, it is cited like a book, with a descriptive title enclosed in brackets. When information is missing, use these abbreviations: *N.p.* for "No place of publication," *n.p.* for "no publisher," and *n.d.* for "no date." None of these abbreviations is italicized in an entry.

Office of Victim Assistance. (2010). *Children affected by crime* [Brochure]. Washington, DC: Author.

> **First in-text citation** (Office of Victim Assistance [OVA], 2010)
>
> **Subsequent citations** (OVA, 2010)

Traumatic brain injury [Brochure]. (2009). Baltimore, MD: U.S. Department of Veteran Affairs, Veterans Health Administration.

> **In-text citation** (*Traumatic Brain Injury*, 2009)

6s   An Unpublished Dissertation

A published dissertation is a book and should be cited accordingly (see 6a). The entry for an unpublished dissertation begins with the author's name, the date, and the title, presented in the pattern used for a book. In parentheses, include the phrase *Unpublished doctoral dissertation* (not italicized), followed by a period. Then provide the name of the degree-granting university, followed by a comma and the city and state (or country) in which the university is located.

Sherriff, G. L. R. (2010). *Stranger than fiction: True crime narratives in contemporary Latin American literature.* (Unpublished doctoral dissertation). Yale University, New Haven, CT.

> **In-text citation** (Sherriff, 2010)

Sperstad, R. A. (2010). *Nursing education: Cultural transformation through guided critical reflection.* (Unpublished doctoral dissertation). University of St. Thomas, St. Paul, MN.

> **In-text citation** (Sperstad, 2010)

6t   Published Proceedings From a Conference

The published proceedings from a conference present revised, printed versions of papers that were delivered at the meeting. If the proceedings are published individually, cite them as books. If they are published regularly, present them as periodicals.

Capitalize the name of the meeting or conference. If the title includes the state, province, or country, do not repeat it in the publishing information.

Holtman, B. (2011). Future challenges and new actors: From crime prevention to safe communities. *Proceedings of ICPC's 15th Anniversary Conference: Crime prevention across the world: Taking stock, evaluation, and future perceptions* (pp. 72–82). Montreal, Canada: International Centre for the Prevention of Crime.

> **In-text citation** (Holtman, 2011)

Keyserling, H. (2011, February 23–24). Immunization of healthcare personnel. In *First international conference on measles immunization* [Conference proceedings] (pp. 57–67). Atlanta, GA: Centers for Disease Control and Prevention.

   In-text citation (Keyserling, 2011)

6u   Multiple Works by the Same Author

When citing several sources by the same author, repeat the name completely each time. Alphabetical order takes precedence, with single authors listed before multiple authors. List works by single authors or by the same multiple authors chronologically. If works are published in the same year, arrange them alphabetically by title.

Sternberg, R. J. (1990). *Metaphors of the mind: Conceptions of the nature of intelligence.* New York, NY: Cambridge University Press.

Sternberg, R. J. (Ed.). (2003). *Psychologists defying the crowd: Stories of those who battled the establishment and won.* Washington, DC: American Psychological Association.

Sternberg, R. J. (2003). *Why smart people can be so stupid.* New Haven, CT: Yale University Press.

Sternberg, R. J. (2007). *Wisdom, intelligence, and creativity synthesized.* New York, NY: Cambridge University Press.

Sternberg, R. J., & Grigorenko, E. L. (2003). *The psychology of abilities, competencies, and expertise.* New York, NY: Cambridge University Press.

Sternberg, R. J., & Grigorenko, E. L. (2007). *Teaching for successful intelligence: To increase student learning and achievement* (2nd ed.). Thousand Oaks, CA: Corwin Press.

Sternberg, R. J., & Preiss, D. D. (Eds.). (2005). *Intelligence and technology: The impact of tools on the nature and development of human abilities.* In *Educational Psychology Series.* New York, NY: Routledge.

   Alternative in-text citations

   The 1990 book: (Sternberg, 1990)

   The first 2003 book: (Sternberg, 2003a)

   The second 2003 book: (Sternberg, 2003b)

   All four single-author works in the same citation: (Sternberg, 1990, 2003a, 2003b, 2007)

   The first multiple-author book: (Sternberg & Grigorenko, 2003)

The second multiple-author book: (Sternberg & Grigorenko, 2007)

The third multiple-author book: (Sternberg & Preiss, 2005)

A combination of sources in the same citation: (Sternberg, 1990, 2007; Sternberg & Grigorenko, 2003)

Sternberg's four separately written works appear first, arranged in chronological order and then alphabetically by title. The Sternberg and Grigorenko books follow, again in chronological order. The Sternberg and Preiss book is last.

6v A Secondary Source

The authors of primary sources report their own research and ideas; the authors of secondary sources report the research and ideas of others. For example, Fisher, Bynum, and Skinner (2009) reported on hospitals' financial practices in an article titled "Getting Past Denial: The High Cost of Health Care in the United States" (*New England Journal of Medicine*); it is a primary source. Aries and Caress (2011) incorporated material from Fisher, Bynum, and Skinner's article in their book chapter "Hospitals: The Power of Institutional Interests"; the chapter is, consequently, a secondary source for the material. Although it is best to use the original or primary source (Fisher, Bynum, & Skinner, 2009), sometimes you must use the secondary source (Aries & Caress, 2011).

Aries, N., & Caress, B. (2011). Hospitals: The power of institutionalized interests. In D. M. Nickitas, D. J. Middaugh, & N. Aries (Eds.), *Policy and politics for nurses and other health professionals* (pp. 123–141). Sudbury, MA: Jones.

In-text commentary and citation

Fisher, Bynum, and Skinner (2009) observed that to remain viable hospitals must both integrate their systems and find additional ways to lower costs (as cited in Aries & Caress, 2011).

Audiovisual sources—motion pictures, recordings, speeches, works of art, and other visual images—are used infrequently in APA papers. Nevertheless, they can provide interesting support for discussions and create variety within a paper.

To cite an audiovisual source in a reference list, follow the guidelines in this chapter.

7a   A Motion Picture

An entry for a motion picture begins with the producer's or director's name (with the word *Producer* or *Director* in parentheses but not italicized), followed by the year of the motion picture's release, its title (italicized, with sentence-style capitalization), and a descriptive title (in brackets). The entry ends with the country of origin and the company.

Include other people's contributions after the motion picture title (in brackets), using brief phrases (*Narr. by, With, Written by*—not italicized) to clarify their roles.

Gigliotti, D., Gordon, J., & Russell, D. O. (Producers), & Russell, D. O. (Director). (2012). *Silver linings playbook* [Motion picture]. [With B. Cooper, J. Lawrence, R. De Niro, & J. Weaver]. United States: The Weinstein Company–Mirage Enterprises.

First in-text citation (Gigliotti, Gordon, & Russell, 2012)

Subsequent citations (Gigliotti et al., 2012)

Lary, B. K. (Producer & Director). (2008). *History of world criminal justice* [Motion picture]. [Written by B. K. Lary, A. Carlton, & M. Westin]. United States: Insight Media.

> **In-text citation** (Lary, 2008)

7b A Slide Set or Filmstrip

A slide set (either photographic slides or those prepared in PowerPoint or other digital formats) or a filmstrip is cited just as a motion picture is, with one exception: Include a descriptive title, such as *Slide set,* in brackets (but not italicized) after the title.

Determined accord: Pandemic preparedness workshop for community managers [Slide set]. (2009). Washington, DC: U.S. Department of Homeland Security–Federal Emergency Management Agency.

> **In-text citation** (*Determined Accord,* 2009)

Because the source had no producer or director, the citation begins with the title. The in-text citation uses a shortened version of the title.

Technical Working Group for Eyewitness Evidence. (2003). *Eyewitness evidence: A trainer's manual for law enforcement* (NCJ 188678) [Slides]. United States: U.S. Department of Justice.

> **First in-text citation** (Technical Working Group for Eyewitness Evidence [TWGEE], 2003)
>
> **Subsequent citations** (TWGEE, 2003)

As a government document, this entry incorporates a publication number after the title of the slide series.

7c A Television Broadcast

A regular television program is listed by producer or director, broadcast date (which may be either a year or a specific broadcast date), program title (italicized, with sentence-style capitalization), a descriptive phrase (in brackets), the city and state (or country), and the network (spelled out completely). Include other people's contributions after the program title (in brackets), using brief phrases (*Narr. by, With, Written by*—not italicized) to clarify their roles.

Newman, L. (Producer). (2010). *Scrubs* [Television series]. [With Z. Braff, D. Faison, M. Mosley, K. Bishé, J. C. McGinley, E. Coupe, & D. Franco]. New York, NY: National Broadcasting Company.

> **In-text citation** (Newman, 2010)

To refer to an individual episode, cite the writer and director, the specific broadcast date, the episode title (with sentence-style capitalization and without special punctuation), and a descriptive phrase in brackets. Introduced by the word *In* (not italicized), the series' executive producer is listed next (his or her name is in normal order, followed by the phrase *Executive Producer* in parentheses, not italicized), followed by a comma. The title of the series follows, along with other standard information.

Winter, T. (Writer), & Van Patten, T. (Director). (2012, September 16). Resolution [Television series episode]. [With S. Buscemi, K. Macdonald, S. Shannon, S. Graham, & B. Cannavale]. In T. Winter, M. Scorsese, M. Wahlberg, T. Van Patten, H. Korder, & S. Levenson (Executive producers), *Boardwalk empire*. Los Angeles, CA: Home Box Office.

In-text citation (Winter & Van Patten, 2012)

Note that only the year appears in the in-text citation.

7d A Radio Broadcast

An entry for a radio broadcast follows the guidelines for a television broadcast; however, note that a radio station's call letters or call numbers are listed. When a broadcast does not have an assigned title, add a descriptive phrase in brackets.

Balancing work, medication, and mental illness [Radio broadcast]. (2012, January 30). In *Talk of the nation*. Washington, DC: NPR.

In-text citation ("Balancing Work," 2012)

Silberner, J. (2011, September 5). Chronic fatigue syndrome still a medical mystery [Radio broadcast]. In *Morning edition*. Washington, DC: NPR.

In-text citation (Silberner, 2011)

7e A Recording

An entry for an entire recording begins with the writer–composer's name, the date of the recording, and the album title (in italics, with sentence-style capitalization), with the recording format in brackets. The entry ends with the city and state (or country), and distribution company.

Winehouse, A. (2006). *Back to black* [CD]. New York, NY: Universal Records.

In-text citation (Winehouse, 2006)

To emphasize a single selection on a recording, begin with the writer–composer and the date, followed by the title of the brief work (with sentence-style capitalization but without special punctuation). Using the word *On* (not italicized), include the title of the complete recording and other production information. Include the track number in the in-text citation.

The Beatles. (2009). Helter skelter. [Written by P. McCartney]. On *The white album* (Remastered) [CD]. Hollywood, CA–London, England: Capital–EMI. (Original work released 1968)

> *In-text citation* (The Beatles, 1968/2009, disc 2, track 6)

A remastered recording, like a revised or reprinted book, requires clarification in parentheses, as well as a parenthetical statement about the original release. Both release dates are included in the in-text citation.

7f An Interview

An interview is a personal communication. As such, it is not included in a reference list. However, it is cited in the text of the paper by enclosing the phrase *personal communication* (not italicized) and the date in parentheses. Notice that initials are required with the name.

Although "correctional education" once meant providing the incarcerated with comprehensive educational experiences (including college-level courses), the current trend is to provide only vocational training; while expedient and cost effective, this shift of focus is extremely short-sighted (L. R. Bates, personal communication, August 16, 2012).

7g A Transcript

A transcript entry describes the source of an original broadcast, with clarifying information in brackets, and information about availability.

Bowser, B. (2011, August 29). Drug hoarders: Manufacturing cuts exacerbate shortage of key medications [Television series episode]. In *PBS newshour* [Transcript]. Washington, DC: Public Broadcasting Service. Available: PBS Transcripts.

> *In-text citation* (Bowser, 2011)

Gupta, S. (2010, April 18). Addiction: Life on the edge. In *CNN presents* [Television series episode]. [Transcript]. Atlanta, GA: Cable News Network. Available: CNN Transcripts.

> *In-text citation* (Gupta, 2010)

7h   A Lecture or Speech

An entry for a lecture or speech includes the speaker's name, the date of the speech, the title of the speech (italicized) or a descriptive title (in brackets), a series title or a description of the speech-making context, and the location (most often, the city and state or country).

Stevens, J. P. (2011, October 11). *A conversation with Justice John Paul Stevens*. Lecture presented for the Public Lecture Series, Princeton University, Princeton, NJ.

> **In-text citation** (Stevens, 2011)

Volkow, N. (2011, April 25). *The neurobiology of drug addiction*. Lecture presented for the Public Lecture Series, Princeton University, Princeton, NJ.

> **In-text citation** (Volkow, 2011)

7i   A Work of Art

An entry for a work of art includes the artist's name, the completion date, the title (either assigned by the artist or attributed), a description of the medium (enclosed in brackets), the city (and state or country) where the museum is located, and the museum or collection name. When artists assign titles, they are italicized; do not italicize titles that other people have assigned to the work.

Hopper, E. (1930). *Early Sunday morning* [Oil on canvas]. New York, NY: Whitney Museum of American Art.

> **In-text citation** (Hopper, 1930)

Warhol, A. (1964). *Electric chair* [Screenprint and acrylic on canvas]. London, England: Tate Modern.

> **In-text citation** (Warhol, 1964)

7j   A Map, Graph, Table, or Chart

Often prepared as part of another source, a map, graph, table, or chart is most often treated like a selection in an edited collection (or a chapter in a book). If known, include the name of the author, artist, or designer responsible for the element, followed by the publication date, in parentheses. Include the title, with sentence-style capitalization but without special punctuation. Follow the title with a descriptive label in brackets, followed by a period. Then include entry information required for the source. When a map, graph, table, or chart is prepared independently, it is treated like a book.

Federal Bureau of Investigation. (2010). Arrests by race, 2006
    [Table]. In S. L. Gabbidon, *Race, ethnicity, crime, and justice: An
    international dilemma* (pp. 74–77). Los Angeles, CA: Sage.

   First in-text citation (Federal Bureau of Investigation
   [FBI], 2010)

   Subsequent citations (FBI, 2010)

Pérez, M. A., & Luquis, R. R. (2008). U.S. population by state,
    density, and distribution, 2006 [Map]. In M. A. Pérez & R. R.
    Luquis (Eds.), *Cultural competence in health education and health
    promotion* (p. 4). San Francisco, CA: Jossey–Bass.

   In-text citation (Pérez & Luquis, 2008)

8 Citing Electronic Sources

The Internet provides researchers with access to an amazing array of resources. Many periodicals are now available in electronic, as well as print, form. Books—out-of-print volumes, as well as recent publications—are accessible online. Documents, correspondence, photographs, films, recordings, and a host of other resource materials are available online in digitized form. Because these sources are available anywhere that a researcher can establish an Internet connection, research is no longer a local activity, restricted to the nearby library, lab, or collection. Instead, researchers can access a far broader range of materials than they once could.

Take advantage of the wealth of online material but be aware that citing these resources sometimes requires ingenuity because citation information can be difficult to locate.

To cite online sources in a reference list, follow the guidelines in this chapter.

Principles for Citing Electronic Sources

1. **Follow patterns for print sources when possible.**
   Use reference-list entries for similar print sources as
   your guide: Include as much of the information that is
   required for corresponding print versions as you can
   locate and present the information in the same order
   and format.

2. **Provide retrieval information.** After providing basic
   information about an online source—author, date, title,
   and so on—add sufficient retrieval information so that
   readers can locate your sources on the Internet. Use
   retrieval dates *only* when sources are likely to change
   (for example, wikis).

3. **Use a digital object identifier (DOI) when available.**
   Current publications usually display the DOI—a fixed
   alphanumeric link to an online document—at the top
   of the first page. When it is available, use it to identify
   the source.

4. **Use a uniform resource locator (URL) as an alternative.**
   When a DOI is not available, use the URL of the home page
   of the online source. A complete URL is necessary *only* when
   a source is difficult to locate within a website.

5. **Present a source's DOI or URL with care.** To ensure
   that you record a DOI or URL exactly, copy and paste it
   into your reference-list entry.

Retrieval Statements

KIND OF SOURCE	*PATTERN FOR RETRIEVAL STATEMENT*
A source with a digital object identifier (DOI)	doi:10.1022/0012-9142.76.3.482
A source with a home page URL	Retrieved from http://troopers.ny.gov
An abstract (a phrase ending in a database name is followed by a period; a phrase ending in a URL has no closing period)	Abstract retrieved from SAGE Journals database. Abstract retrieved from http://www.ncjrs.gov
A source from an organizational or professional website	Retrieved from the Bureau of Justice Statistics website: http://bjs.ojp.usdoj.gov

6. **Divide the DOI or URL when necessary**. To avoid large spaces in citations, divide DOIs or URLs *before* punctuation; however, retain *http://* as a unit.

7. **Present retrieval statements with care**. A retrieval statement ending with a DOI or a URL has no end punctuation because a closing period might be misinterpreted as part of the identification number or electronic address.

As you gather information to cite electronic sources, your goal should be to provide the most complete set of information possible for each electronic source, following the guidelines in this chapter.

Specialized Online Sources

Online sources exist in many forms. Although they are all designed in approximately the same way—with a home page that directs users to subpages where information can be found—some specialized sites have distinct purposes and applications.

- **Professional websites.** Affiliated with professional organizations, these sites provide materials that support or enhance the work of the organization—research documents, online resources, web links, news items, press releases, and so on. Website titles typically include the organization's name, but if they do not, this information may be added for clarity.

- **Information databases.** Typically developed by information-technology firms or governmental agencies, these sites provide access to cataloged information that is accessed by using keyword search terms. Periodical databases like ProQuest, EBSCOhost, LexisNexis, JSTOR, and WorldCat make periodical articles available in a variety of formats; other databases provide access to cataloged recordings, images, historical documents, and so on. When the database name is included in a URL, it does not have to be listed separately in a reference-list entry; however, when the URL includes only an acronym, it is often helpful to provide the name for additional clarity.

- **Scholarly projects.** Often affiliated with universities, foundations, and government agencies, these sites are depositories of resources as varied as articles, books, digitized images of original documents, sound recordings, and film clips. Because their affiliations help establish their credibility, that information is sometimes included in reference-list entries.

8a   An Article in an Online Journal

To cite an article in an online journal, first provide the information that is required for the print version of the article (see 5a and 5b). Then close the entry with a retrieval statement. If the article has a DOI, use it. If it does not, present a retrieval statement that is appropriate for the kind of online source (see page 102).

Orth, U., Trzesniewski, K. H., & Robbins, R. W. (2010). Self-esteem development from young adulthood to old age: A cohort-sequential longitudinal study. *Journal of Personality and Social Psychology, 98,* 645–658. doi: 10.1037/a0018769

First in-text citation (Orth, Trzesniewski, & Robbins, 2010)

Subsequent citations (Orth et al., 2010)

Yehia, B., & Frank, I. (2011). Battling AIDS in America: An evaluation of the national HIV/AIDS strategy. *American Journal of Public Health, 111,* E4–E8. doi: 10.2105/AJPH.2011.300259

In-text citation (Yehia & Frank, 2011)

8b   An Article in an Online Magazine

Articles in online magazines are presented in the same ways as those in online journals, except that dates may also include days and months (see 5d and 5e). Then present a retrieval statement that is appropriate for the kind of online source (see page 102).

Fitzpatrick, L. (2010, February 23). The death penalty: Racist, classist, and unfair. *Time.* Retrieved from http://www.time.com

In-text citation (Fitzpatrick, 2010)

Miller, G. (2010, May). How our brains make memories. *Smithsonian.* Retrieved from http://www.smithsonianmag.com

In-text citation (Miller, 2010)

8c   An Article in an Online Newspaper

To cite an article in an online newspaper, first provide the information that is required for the print version of the article (see 5f) but exclude section designations and page numbers. Then present a retrieval statement that is appropriate for the kind of online source (see page 102).

Dance, A. (2011, August 22). Therapeutic hypothermia: Keeping cool in emergencies. *Los Angeles Times.* Retrieved from http://www.latimes.com

In-text citation (Dance, 2011)

Hax, C. (2012, December 10). Working up the courage to get
    counseling for depression. *Washington Post*. Retrieved from
    http://www.washingtonpost.com

    In-text citation (Hax, 2012)

8d   An Article in an Online Newsletter

An entry for an online newsletter follows the same pattern as that
for an online newspaper (see 5g). Then present a retrieval statement that is appropriate for the kind of online source (see page
102); if a newsletter article is difficult to locate within the source,
include the complete URL.

Laub, J. H. (2011, March/April). Moving the National Institute
    of Justice forward. *The Criminologist*. Retrieved from
    the American Society of Criminology website:
    http://www.asc41.com

    In-text citation (Laub, 2011)

Waking up to anesthesia: Learning more before you go under.
    (2011, April). *NIH News in Health*. Retrieved from
    http://www.newsinhealth.nih.gov

    In-text citation ("Waking Up," 2011)

8e   An Online Book

To cite an online book, first prepare a standard entry (see 6a to 6q);
however, omit the city and publisher. Then present a retrieval
statement that is appropriate for the kind of online source
(see page 102).

Pierce, R. V. (1895). *The people's common sense medical advisor
    in plain English, or medicine simplified* (54th ed.). Retrieved from
    http://www.gutenberg.org/catalog

    In-text citation (Pierce, 1895)

Treverton, G. F. (2008). *Reorganizing U.S. domestic intelligence:
    Assessing the options* (Rand Monographs). Retrieved from www
    .rand.org

    In-text citation (Treverton, 2008)

8f   An Online Dissertation or Thesis

To cite an online dissertation or thesis, include author, date, and title, followed by the phrase *Doctoral dissertation* or *Master's thesis* (not
italicized) in parentheses. Close the entry with a retrieval statement

that includes the name of the database and, if available, the accession or order number in parentheses.

Blandon, K. C. (2011). Brain, psyche, and self: A dialectic between analytic psychology and neuroscience (Doctoral dissertation). Available from ProQuest Dissertations and Theses database. (UMI No. 3519792)

> **In-text citation** (Blandon, 2011)

Ndayishimiye, J. (2011). Differential equations modeling of patients and physicians dynamics in emergency rooms: Optimal control policies and heuristic implementation (Doctoral dissertation). Available from ProQuest Dissertations and Theses database. (UMI No. 1488979)

> **In-text citation** (Ndayishimiye, 2011)

8g   An Online Abstract

To cite an abstract of an article in an online journal or an abstract from an online service, first provide the information that is required for the print version of an abstract (see 5c). Then provide a retrieval statement that is appropriate for your source; you may include an accession number in parentheses at the end of the entry.

Der Pau, P. J., Deng, L. F., Chang, S. S. H., & Jiang, K. T. (2011). Correctional officers' perceptions of a solution-focused training program: Potential implications for working with offenders [Abstract]. *International Journal of Offender Therapy and Comparative Criminology, 55,* 863–879. doi: 10.1177/0306624X10378231

> **First in-text citation** (Der Pau, Deng, Change, & Jiang, 2011)
>
> **Subsequent citations** (Der Pau et al., 2011)

McKillip, J., Courtney, C. L., Locasso, R., Eckert, P., & Holly, F. (2010). College students' use of emergency medical services [Abstract]. *Journal of American College Health, 38,* 289–292. Abstract retrieved from http://www.informationworld.com

> **First in-text citation** (McKillip, Courtney, Locasso, Eckert, & Holly, 2010)
>
> **Subsequent citations** (McKillip et al., 2010)

8h   An Article in an Online Encyclopedia or Other Reference Work

To cite an article from an online encyclopedia or reference work, first provide the information required for a print source (see 6l). Then include a retrieval statement (see page 102).

Intelligence. (2012). In *Merriam–Webster's online dictionary*.
   Retrieved from http://www.merriam-webster.com/dictionary/
   In-text citation ("Intelligence," 2012)

Karmen, A. (2011). Victimology. In *Britannica online encyclopedia*.
   Retrieved from http://britannica.com
   In-text citation (Karmen, 2011)

8i   A Professional Website, Information Database, or Scholarly Project

If you refer to an entire professional website, information database, or scholarly project, you do not need to include an entry in your reference list. However, you must identify the title of the source clearly in the text of your paper (capitalized but without special punctuation) and provide the electronic address in parentheses, as in this sample:

   In addition to membership services, the American Psychological Association website includes several extremely useful subpages for general readers—including "Psychology Topics," which addresses subjects ranging from ADHD to workplace issues, and "Psychological Help Center," which provides brief articles, lists of suggestions, and blogs (http://www.apa.org).

   To cite a source—an article, illustration, map, or other element—from a professional website, information database, or scholarly project, include the author (or artist, compiler, or editor) of the individual source, if available; the date; and the title of the source, without special punctuation. The retrieval statement includes the name of the website, database, or project (not italicized), a colon, and the site's URL. However, if a website's name is clear from the URL, it is not required in the retrieval statement.

Johnson, D. (2011, September 1). Measles case abroad linked to the increase of the disease in U.S.: Resurgence shows need for vaccinations. Retrieved from the American Public Health Association website: http://www.apha.org
   In-text citation (Johnson, 2011)

Treating offenders with drug problems: Integrating public health and public safety. (2011). Retrieved from the National Institute on Drug Abuse website: http://www.nida.nih.gov
   In-text citation ("Treating Offenders," 2011)

8j   An Online Transcript of a Lecture or Speech

To cite an online transcript of a lecture or speech, first provide the information required for a lecture or a speech (see 7h). Then include the word *Transcript,* not italicized and in brackets, and a retrieval statement that is appropriate for the kind of online source (see page 102).

Darrow, C. (1924, August 22). [Summary defense for Leopold & Loeb]. Speech presented in U.S. District Court, New York, NY. [Transcript]. Retrieved from http://www.americanrhetoric.com

> *In-text citation* (Darrow, 1924)

Johnson, L. B. (1965, July 30). [Speech]. Remarks at the signing of the Medicare Bill, Independence, MO. [Transcript]. Retrieved from the Lyndon Baines Johnson Library and Museum website: http://www.lbjlibrary.org

> *In-text citation* (Johnson, 1965)

8k   An Online Map, Graph, Table, or Chart

To cite an online map, graph, table, or chart, first provide the information required for the kind of visual element (see 7j). Then present a retrieval statement that is appropriate for the kind of online source (see page 102).

Centers for Disease Control and Prevention. (2011). Frequency distributions of current cigarette smoking status among persons 18 years or over, by selected characteristics: United States, 2008 [Table]. Retrieved from the Centers for Disease Control and Prevention website: http://www.cdc.gov

> *First in-text citation* (Centers for Disease Control and Prevention [CDC], 2011)

> *Subsequent citations* (CDC, 2011)

Although logic might suggest that the acronym would be *CDCP*, the organization continues to use the shorter, more familiar form: *CDC*.

Federal Bureau of Investigation. (2011). Bank crime statistics: January 1, 2010–December 31, 2010 [Table]. Retrieved from the Federal Bureau of Investigation website: http://www.fbi.gov

> *First in-text citation* (Federal Bureau of Investigation [FBI], 2011)

> *Subsequent citations* (FBI, 2011)

8l A CD-ROM Source

To cite a CD-ROM source, include the author or editor, the release date, and the title, italicized. End the entry with the following information in parentheses: the publisher or distributor; the word *CD-ROM,* not italicized; the release date; and an item number, if applicable.

Centers for Disease Control and Prevention. (2003). *International classification of diseases* (6th ed.). (U.S. Government Printing Office, CD-ROM, 2003 release).

> **First in-text citation** (Centers for Disease Control and Prevention [CDC], 2003)
>
> **Subsequent citations** (CDC, 2003)

Schmalleger, F. T. (2008). *Criminal justice simulations* (10th ed.). (Pearson–Prentice Hall, CD-ROM, 2008 release).

> **In-text citation** (Schmalleger, 2008)

8m An E-Mail Interview

An interview conducted through e-mail correspondence is considered personal communication. As such, it is not included in the reference list. However, it is cited in the text of the paper by enclosing the phrase *personal communication* (not italicized) and the date of the e-mail in parentheses.

Murray (personal communication, September 9, 2012) noted that while electronic diagnostics can improve record keeping, patients often resent clinicians keying in data during consultations.

8n An Online Video Podcast

To cite an online video podcast, provide the information required for regularly distributed motion pictures or television broadcasts (see 7a or 7c). Then present a retrieval statement that is appropriate for the kind of online source (see page 102).

Rich, J. (2010, January 6). Wrong place, wrong time: Understanding trauma and violence in the lives of young black men [Video podcast]. Retrieved from the National Institutes of Health website: http://www.nih.gov

> **In-text citation** (Rich, 2010)

World Health Organization. (2011, August). *Unite in the fight against NCDs* [Video podcast]. Retrieved from the World Health Organization website: http://www.who.int

First in-text citation (World Health Organization [WHO], 2011)

Subsequent citations (WHO, 2011)

8o   An Online Audio Podcast

To cite an online audio podcast, provide the information required for regular radio broadcasts, recordings, or speeches (7d, 7e, or 7h). Then present a retrieval statement that is appropriate for the kind of online source (see page 102).

Johnson, C. (2011, April 20). After financial crisis, wheels of justice turn slowly [Audio podcast]. In *All things considered*. Retrieved from http://www.npr.org

In-text citation (Johnson, 2011)

Kastenbaum, S. (2010, May 6). A family fights back [Audio podcast]. In *CNN radio reports*. Retrieved from http://www.cnn.com/services/podcasting

In-text citation (Kastenbaum, 2010)

8p   An Online Posting—Blog
or Discussion Group

To cite an online posting to a blog or discussion group, provide the author, identified by name or screen name; the date of the posting; the title of the posting, with a description of the message; and a retrieval statement that is appropriate for the kind of online source (see page 102).

Molitor, N. (2012, May 24). TV psychotherapy often gets it wrong [Blog message]. Retrieved from the American Psychological Association website: http://www.apa.org

In-text citation (Molitor, 2012)

Suarez, R. (2011, September 8). The silent, deadly epidemic of non-communicative disease [Blog message]. Retrieved from the Public Broadcasting Service website: http://www.pbs.org

In-text citation (Suarez, 2011)

Running head: BEYOND BIRTH ORDER   1

Labeled
running head:
all capitals (35)

Beyond Birth Order:
Recognizing Other Variables
Elissa Allen
Indiana State University

Identifying
information:
centered
(25–26)

If an author
note is
required, it
appears at the
bottom of the
title page (26).

BEYOND BIRTH ORDER   2

Abstract

Although scholars continue to make a case for birth-order effects in children's development, exclusive reliance on this useful but one-dimensional criterion ignores other variables that affect children's personal, intellectual, and social development. The sex of other siblings, the time between births, the size of the family, the age of the mother, the psychological condition of the children, the absence of a parent, and the birth order of the parents also influence a child's development.

Centered label
with normal
capitalization
(27)

Unindented ¶:
250 words or
fewer (27)

BEYOND BIRTH ORDER   3

The text begins on page 3 (27–28).

Beyond Birth Order:

Recognizing Other Variables

Sigmund Freud, Queen Elizabeth II, Albert Einstein, William Shakespeare, George Washington, Jacqueline Kennedy, John Milton, Julius Caesar, Leontyne Price, and Winston Churchill. What do these famous people have in common? They were all first-born children. The fact that so many important people in all spheres of influence have been first-born children lends credence to the notion that birth order helps determine the kind of people we become.

Centered title with headline-style capitalization (28)

Allusions as an introductory strategy

Historical context established

Scientific studies over the years have, in fact, suggested that birth order affects an individual's development. For example, Pine (1995) suggested that first-born children acquire language skills sooner than later-born children. Skinner and Fox-Francoeur (2010) observed that first-born children use established procedures to solve problems, whereas later-born children use less predictable strategies. Kluger (2007) noted that later-born children are more inclined toward risky activities than are first-born children, and Sulloway (1995) observed that later-born children are more rebellious than first-born children. Further, Ernst and Angst (1983) explained the underlying premise of birth-order effects this way: "Everybody agrees that birth-order differences must arise from differential socialization by the parents. There is, however, no general theory on how this differential socialization actually works" (p. x). Yet other studies (Eckstein & Kaufman, 2012; Herrera, Zajonc, Wieczorkowska, & Cichomski, 2003;

Past tense to describe scholarship (52)

General reference: author and date (67)

Specific reference: author, date, and page (70)

BEYOND BIRTH ORDER 4

Salmon, Shackelford, & Michalski, 2012)
suggested that parents' beliefs about birth-order
differences influence their expectations for their
children. Stein (2008) also observed that
birth-order effects are more pronounced in families
that are competitive and democratic, and Carette,
Anseel, and Van Yperen (2011) noted that birth
order establishes varied levels of emphasis on goal
setting (first born) and on winning (last born). It is
not surprising, then, that a general theory has not
emerged because many other variables besides
birth order influence an individual's personal,
intellectual, and social development.

Thesis statement (2–3)

Sex of the Siblings

While acknowledging that birth order plays a
part in an individual's development, scholars have
begun to recognize that it is only one variable. For
example, Sutton-Smith and Rosenberg (1970)
observed that even in two-child families there are
four possible variations for sibling relationships
based on gender: (a) first-born female, second-born
female; (b) first-born female, second-born male;
(c) first-born male, second-born male; (c) first-born
male, second-born female. In families with three
children, the variations increase to 24. To suggest
that being the first-born child is the same in all of
these contexts ignores too many variables.

Headings to divide the discussion (35–36)

Elements in a series (34)

Common knowledge suggests that the number increases to 24 (17–18).

Time Between Births

Forer (1976) suggested that when the births
of children are separated by 5 or more years, the
effects of birth order are changed. For example,

Summary of Forer's ideas

BEYOND BIRTH ORDER   5

in a family with four children (with children aged 12, 6, 4, and 2 years old), the second child would be more likely to exhibit the characteristics of an oldest child because of his or her nearness in age to the younger children and the 6-year separation in age from the oldest child. The pattern would differ from that of a sibling in a four-child family if the children were spaced fewer than 3 years apart (for example, if the children were 10, 8, 5, and 3 years old); this second child would exhibit the characteristics typical of a second–middle child.

Size of Family

Studies have also suggested that the size of the family modifies the effects of birth order (Kanazawa, 2012; Kristensen & Bjerkedal, 2007). In a moderate-sized family (two to four children), the first-born child usually achieves the highest level of education; however, Forer (1969) observed that "a first-born child from a large family has often been found to obtain less education than a last-born child from such a family" (p. 24). Whether this occurs because large families tend to have lower socioeconomic status or whether it is the result of varied family dynamics, the overall size of the family seems to alter the preconceived notions of birth order and its influence on a child's development (Hartshorne, 2010).

Age of the Mother

Studies have suggested that a mother's age has a strong bearing on the child's learned behavior, regardless of birth order (Bonesrønning & Massih,

Comparative numbers in the same form (49)

Elissa's own example: no documentation required

Last names of authors only

BEYOND BIRTH ORDER   6

2011; Booth & Kee, 2009). Sutton-Smith and
Rosenberg (1970) offered this perspective:

> On a more obvious level, younger mothers have
> more stamina and vigor than older mothers. One
> speculation in the literature is that they are also
> more anxious and uncertain about their child-
> training procedures, and that this has an effect of
> inducing anxiety in their offspring. (p. 138)

Long quotation: 5-space indentation (71–72)

Set-in (block) quotation: period before the citation (71–72)

It seems safe to assume, then, that the third child
of a woman of 28 will have a different experience
growing up than the third child of a woman of
39. They may share the same relational patterns
with their siblings, but they will not share the
same patterns with their mothers.

Psychological Factors

Early studies on birth order failed to account
for psychological differences among children,
even among those who shared the same birth
status. Forer (1969) asserted, however, that
"special conditions involving a child in a family
may change the birth-order effect both for him
and his siblings" (p. 19). Conditions such as a
child's mental retardation, severe hearing loss,
blindness, handicaps—or even exceptional beauty,
intelligence, or physical skill—can alter the
dynamics of the family and consequently affect
the traditionally described effects of birth order
(Forer, p. 19). In short, a middle child whose
physiological conditions are outside the normal
spectrum—because of different potential and
opportunity—will not have the same life experiences
as a middle child who is considered average.

Summary of ideas

BEYOND BIRTH ORDER   7

Absence of a Parent

Parents may be absent from family units for a variety of reasons: A parent may die, creating a permanent void in a family unit; a parent may be gone to war or be hospitalized for an extended period, creating a temporary but still notable disruption in the family; or a parent may travel for business, creating an irregular but obvious interruption in the family's normal workings. The loss of a parent can affect a child's experiences and can, under certain circumstances, mitigate the effects of birth order (Sulloway, 1997). Toman (1993) explained that the effects of parental absence will be greater

A long quote
(71–72)

a. The more recently they have occurred,
b. The earlier in a person's life they have occurred,
c. The older the person lost is (in relation to the oldest family member),
d. The longer the person has lived together with the lost person,
e. The smaller the family,
f. The greater the imbalance of the sexes in the family resulting from the loss,
g. The longer it takes the family to find a replacement for the lost person,
h. The greater the number of losses, and the graver the losses, that have occurred before. (pp. 41–42)

Such disruptions—whether major or minor—alter the family unit and often have a greater influence on the children than the traditional effects of birth order.

BEYOND BIRTH ORDER   8

Birth Order of Parents

A number of scholars have asserted that the birth order of parents influences to a high degree their interrelationships with their children and, consequently, creates an impact that extends beyond the simple birth order of the children. Toman (1993) described the family relationships, based on birth order, that promise the least conflict and, consequently, best situation for children's development:

> If the mother is the youngest sister of a brother and has an older son and a younger daughter, she can identify with her daughter and the daughter with the mother. The daughter, too, is the younger sister of a brother. Moreover, the mother has no trouble dealing with her son, for she had an older brother in her original family and her son, too, is an older brother of a sister. (p. 199)

Toman's assumption that parents relate better to their children when they have shared similar sibling-related experiences leads to this assumption: When parents can create a positive and productive home environment (because of familiar familial relationships), the children will benefit. When conflict occurs because sibling relations are unfamiliar, everyone suffers. Parent–child relationships—determined, at least in part, by the parents' own birth orders—would consequently vary from family to family, even when children of those families share the same birth order.

BEYOND BIRTH ORDER   9

Conclusion

According to U.S. Census information collected from 92,119 randomly selected mothers, 28% of children are first born, 28% second born, 20% middle born, and 18% youngest born (as cited in Simpson, Bloom, Newlon, & Arminio, 1994). As long as census takers, scholars, family members, parents, and children think in terms of birth order, we will have an oversimplified perspective of why children develop as they do. Yet studies (Parish, 1990) have suggested that adolescents recognize that family structure and personal interaction have a stronger bearing on their perceptions of themselves, other family members, and their families than does either birth order or even gender. And, importantly, websites such as Matthias Romppel's Birth Order Research (2011) approach the issue cautiously, suggesting that birth-order effects on children are changeable (http://www.romppel.de/birth-order). Perhaps we should take our cues from these young people and current scholars and recognize that birth order is but one interesting variable in personality development.

Percentages in numeral-symbol form (49)

Multiple authors: joined by an ampersand (63)

A reference to a complete website occurs in the paper but does not appear in the reference list (107).

BEYOND BIRTH ORDER 10

References

Bonesrønning, H., & Massih, S. S. (2011). Birth order effects on young students' academic achievement. *Journal of Socio-Economics, 40,* 824–832.

Booth, A. L., & Kee, H. J. (2009). Birth order matters: The effect of family size and birth order on educational attainment. *Journal of Population Economics, 22,* 367–397. doi: 10.1007/s00148-007-0181-4

Carette, B., Anseel, F., & Van Yperen, N. W. (2011). Born to learn or born to win? Birth order effects on achievement goals. *Journal of Research on Personality, 45,* 500–503.

Eckstein, D., & Kaufman, J. A. (2012). The role of birth order in personality: An enduring intellectual legacy of Alfred Adler. *Journal of Individual Psychology, 68*(1), 60–75.

Ernst, C., & Angst, J. (1983). *Birth order: Its influence on personality.* Berlin, Germany: Springer.

Forer, L. K. (1969). *Birth order and life roles.* Springfield, IL: Thomas.

Forer, L. K. (1976). *The birth order factor: How your personality is influenced by your place in the family.* New York, NY: McKay.

Hartshorne, J. K. (2010). Ruled by birth order? *Scientific American Mind, 20*(7), 18–19.

Herrera, N. C., Zajonc, R. B., Wieczorkowska, G., & Cichomski, B. (2003). Beliefs about birth rank and their reflection in reality. *Journal of Personality and Social Psychology 85*(1), 142–150. doi:10.1037/0022-3514.85.1.142

Sequential page numbers (29)

Descriptive title: centered (59)

Journal and book titles italicized, not underlined (48)

Two or more works by same author (66)

A DOI is used instead of a full retrieval statement (102).

BEYOND BIRTH ORDER   11

Kanazawa, S. (2012). Intelligence, birth order, and family size. *Personality and Social Psychology Bulletin, 38,* 1157–1164.

Kluger, J. (2007, October 29). The power of birth order. *Time, 170*(18), 42–48.

Kristensen, P., & Bjerkedal, T. (2007, 22 June). Explaining the relation between birth order and intelligence. *Science, 316,* 1717.

Parish, T. S. (1990). Evaluations of family by youth: Do they vary as a function of family structure, gender, and birth order? *Adolescence, 25,* 353–356.

Pine, J. M. (1995). Variations in vocabulary development as a function of birth order. *Child Development, 66,* 272–281.

Salmon, C. A., Shackelford, T. K., & Michalski, R. L. (2012). Birth order, sex of child, and perceptions of parental favoritism. *Personality and Individual Differences, 52,* 357–362. doi: 10.1016/j.paid.2011.10.033

Simpson, P. W., Bloom, J. W., Newlon, B. J., & Arminio, L. (1994). Birth-order proportions of the general population in the United States. *Individual Psychology: Journal of Adlerian Theory, 50,* 173–182.

Skinner, N. F., & Fox-Francoeur, C. A. (2010). Personality implications of adaption–innovation: Birth order as a determinant of cognitive style. *Social Behavior and Personality, 38,* 237–240. doi: 10.2224/sbp.2010.38.2.237

Stein, H. T. (2008). Adlerian overview of birth order characteristics. Retrieved from the Alfred Adler Institutes of San Francisco

First lines at the normal margin; subsequent lines indented (62)

BEYOND BIRTH ORDER　12

website: http://ourworld.compuserve.com/
homepages/hstein/birthord.htm

Sulloway, F. J. (1995). Birth order and evolutionary
psychology: A meta-analytic overview.
Psychological Inquiry, 6(1), 75–80.

Sulloway, F. J. (1997). *Born to rebel: Birth order,
family dynamics, and creative lives.* New York,
NY: Vintage Books.

Sutton-Smith, B., & Rosenberg, B. G. (1970). *The
sibling.* New York, NY: Holt.

Toman, W. (1993). *Family constellation: Its effects on
personality and social behavior.* New York, NY:
Springer

Labeled
running head:
all capitals
(35)

Identifying
information:
centered
(25–26)

If an author
note is re-
quired, it ap-
pears at the
bottom of the
title page (26).

Students' Reactions to Kinds of Test Questions:
A Piece of the Test-Anxiety Puzzle
Gabriel Stevenson
Indiana State University

Centered label
with normal
capitalization
(27)

Unindented ¶:
250 words or
fewer (27)

Abstract

The purpose of this brief study was to determine
whether specific kinds of test questions produced
anxiety in students. The results of a survey of 89
high school ninth graders indicate that true/false,
multiple-choice, and matching are low-anxiety
question formats, whereas essay, fill-in-the-blank,
and listing are high-anxiety question formats.
However, the study revealed that students' anxiety
levels related to question types do not vary
dramatically, either by question type or by
students' performance levels, as indicated by
previous grades.

STUDENTS' REACTIONS   3

Students' Reactions to Kinds of Test Questions:
A Piece in the Test-Anxiety Puzzle

Today's students are faced with an increasing number of tests. Not only do they take tests for their individual classes, but they also take state-mandated competency tests to progress through school and standardized achievement tests to gain admission to colleges and universities. With the emphasis currently being placed on tests, it is no wonder that many students are now experiencing test anxiety.

One area, however, has not received sufficient attention: students' reactions to specific kinds of test questions. Consequently, using data collected from a sampling of high school students, this brief study attempts to discover with what types of test questions students are most comfortable and what kinds of questioning techniques produce the greatest amount of insecurity or anxiety.

The nature of students' test anxiety has been—and continues to be—studied by scholars in education, psychology, and related fields. By understanding the forms, causes, and results of test anxiety, they hope to provide the means for students and educators to address the problem in helpful ways.

Scholars have noted that shifting cultural contexts—which require the regular use of competency tests—have contributed to increased test anxiety among students (Embse & Hasson, 2012; Spielberger & Vagg, 1995). Other scholars have described the nature of test anxiety, providing

The text begins on page 3 (27–28).

Centered title with headline-style capitalization (28)

Unlabeled introduction: contextualizes the paper, clarifies the topic (28)

Literature review as part of introduction (28)

STUDENTS' REACTIONS   4

useful categories and explanations to enhance the understanding of this multifaceted problem (Bower, 2011; Eum & Rice, 2011; Wigfield & Eccles, 1989). Others have contextualized the testing situation by describing the high-stakes educational environments in which tests are given (Cizek & Burg, 2006; Hancock, 2001).

Scholars have also explored the cognitive processes that are related to test anxiety. Schutz, Davis, and Schwanenflugel (2002) have distinguished between high and low levels of test anxiety and have discussed the ways students perceive the test-taking process and the ways they cope. Others have addressed students' self-awareness about the emotional nature of the testing process and their own procedures for handling emotion during testing (Weiner, 1994; Zeidner, 1995a, 1995b, 2007). Birenbaum (2007) has extended discussions of test anxiety to incorporate students' instructional preferences and learning strategies.

Yet other scholars have discussed test anxiety among special student populations, noting that test anxiety among students with disabilities can lead to poor test performance, lead to poor overall academic performance, and create low self-esteem (Sena, Lowe, & Lee, 2007; Swanson & Howell, 1996). Further, Nelson, Jayanthi, Epstein, and Bursuck (2000) have presented information on alternatives to and adaptations of traditional testing that can allow special-needs students to demonstrate what they know without the additional burden of test anxiety.

Multiple references, separated by semicolons (69)

STUDENTS' REACTIONS 5

These studies have laid a contextual groundwork for further study. In particular, Salend (2011, 2012) has addressed practical issues of test design, such as organization, formatting, and length. However, no studies have addressed whether question types contribute directly to test anxiety. This brief, survey-based study may advance this work in a small but important way.

Method

Participants

The survey group was composed of 89 ninth grade students (44 females and 45 males) from three classes. The students were enrolled in a required (and untracked) ninth-grade English class that included students of varied abilities at a consolidated high school in west-central Indiana. The students had completed one grading period; their grades from the previous term ranged from *A* to *F*.

Materials

Students were given a brief questionnaire (see Appendix) that included these elements: (a) an element to determine gender, (b) an element to record their grades in English during the previous 9 weeks, and (c) a six-element questionnaire using a Likert-type scale so that students could indicate their anxiety-related responses to six types of test questions.

Procedures

The students' teacher distributed the questionnaire at the beginning of each of the

Level-1 headings for major subtopics (35)

"Method" subsection: level-2 headings (35–36)

In-text reference to an appendix (32–33)

Description of materials and procedures (28)

STUDENTS' REACTIONS 6

three class periods and read the instructions aloud, emphasizing that students should respond to the types of questions based on their entire testing experiences, not just those on English tests. Students were then given 10 minutes to complete the questionnaire; most completed the questionnaires in fewer than 5 minutes.

Results

"Results" section: summarizes the data (28)

The most general analysis of the data involved computing students' ratings of question types using the Likert-type scale (1–2 = *secure*, 3–4 = *no reaction*, 5–6 = *insecure*). Percentages of students' responses appear in Table 1.

In-text reference to a table (30–31)

Low-Anxiety Question Types

The findings indicated that true/false test questions created the least anxiety, with 31.4% of students giving them a 1 rating; in addition, 81.9% rated true/false as a 1, 2, or 3, indicating little anxiety. Matching and multiple-choice questions also achieved low anxiety ratings, with 25.8% of students giving them a 1 rating; 79.7% rated matching as a 1, 2, or 3, indicating little anxiety. Interestingly, 84.3% rated multiple-choice questions as a 1, 2, or 3, making multiple choice the question type that produces the least anxiety in the greatest percentage of students.

Subsection: level-2 headings (35–36)

High-Anxiety Question Types

The findings indicated that essay questions created the most anxiety, with 49.4% of students giving them a 6 rating; further, 71.9% rated essay

STUDENTS' REACTIONS   7

questions as a 4, 5, or 6, indicating a high degree
of anxiety. Fill-in-the-blank questions also
achieved a high-anxiety rating, with 24.6% of
students giving them a 6 rating; 65.1% rated
fill-in-the-blank questions as a 4, 5, or 6,
indicating a high degree of anxiety. Finally, 21.4%
of students rated listing questions as a 6; 65.3%
rated them as a 4, 5, or 6, making this a
high-stress question type.

> The summary correlates with tables or figures.

Mean Responses

The mean responses to the question types
(1–2 = *secure*, 3–4 = *no reaction*, 5–6 = *insecure*)
correlated with the individual low-anxiety and
high-anxiety ratings given by students, as shown
in Figure 1. True/false (2.35), multiple-choice
(2.43), and matching (2.53) remained in the
low-anxiety category, but multiple-choice and
matching reversed their rating order. Essay (4.56),
fill-in-the-blank (4.27), and listing (4.16)
remained in the high-anxiety category; they
retained the same rating order.

> In-text reference to a figure (31–32)

As Figure 1 illustrates, mean responses by
students' grade categories showed slightly varied
preferences among high-performing and low-
performing students: *A* students (1: matching; 2:
multiple-choice; 3: true/false; 4: fill-in-the-blank;
5–6: listing and essay), *B* students (1: multiple-
choice; 2: matching; 3: true/false; 4: listing; 5–6:
fill-in-the-blank and essay), *C* students (1: matching;
2: multiple-choice; 3: true/false; 4–5: fill-in-the-blank
and listing; 6: essay), *D* students (1: true/false;

2: multiple-choice; 3: matching; 4: listing; 5: fill-in-the-blank; 6: essay), and *F* students (1: true/false; 2: multiple-choice; 3: matching; 4: listing; 5: fill-in-the-blank; 6: essay).

An average of the mean responses to all six question types for each grade category indicated an increasing degree of anxiety: for *A* students, the averaged mean response was 2.75; for *B* students, 3.08; for *C* students, 3.57; for *D* students, 3.61; and for *F* students, 3.83. Although the increments were small, there was a steady progression from one student group to the next; however, none of the averaged means fell far from the 3–4 range (*no reaction*), suggesting that, generally, no question format made students as a group feel either very secure or very anxious.

Discussion

The data indicate that, for students, question types fall into two distinct groups: low-stress questions (true/false, multiple-choice, matching) and high-stress questions (listing, fill-in-the-blank, essay). However, the data also indicate that, on average, students' anxiety levels related to question types do not vary greatly (mean responses ranged from 2.75 for *A* students to 3.83 for *F* students), which suggests that although question-related anxiety exists, it is not dramatic.

An analysis of the data further indicates that low-anxiety questions (true/false, multiple-choice, matching) are format based, providing information and allowing students to select among options.

"Discussion" section: comments on the data, correlates with the hypothesis (29)

STUDENTS' REACTIONS   9

In contrast, high-anxiety questions (listing, fill-in-the-blank, essay) are open-ended, requiring students to recall and arrange information on their own.

The results of this brief study are, of course, tentative and need to be reproduced with a larger, more comprehensive sample. However, the study does suggest the value of analyzing specific question formats because they can contribute in a small but significant way to overall test anxiety.

A comment on the value of the study (29)

STUDENTS' REACTIONS   10

References

Birenbaum, M. (2007). Assessment and instruction preferences and their relationship with test anxiety and learning strategies. *Higher Education, 53,* 749–768. doi: 10.1007/s10734-005-4843-4

Bower, B. (2011). The write stuff for test anxiety. *Science News, 179*(4), 9.

Cizek, J. C., & Burg, S. S. (2006). *Addressing test anxiety in a high-stakes environment.* Thousand Oaks, CA: Corwin Press.

Embse, N., & Hasson, R. (2012). Test anxiety and high-stakes test performance between school settings: Implications for education. *Preventing School Failure, 56*(3), 180–187.

Eum, K. U., & Rice, K. G. (2011). Test anxiety, perfectionism, goal orientation, and academic performance. *Anxiety, Stress, and Coping, 24,* 167–178.

Hancock, D. R. (2001). Effects of test anxiety and evaluative threat on students' achievement and motivation. *The Journal of Educational Research, 94,* 284–290.

Nelson, J. S., Jayanthi, M., Epstein, M. H., & Bursuck, W. D. (2000). Student preferences for adaptations in classroom testing. *Remedial and Special Education, 21*(1), 41–52.

Salend, S. J. (2011). Addressing test anxiety. *Teaching Exceptional Children, 44*(2), 58–68.

Salend, S. J. (2012). Teaching students not to sweat the test: Teachers can change some of their practices to ensure that students don't feel extreme anxiety at exam time. *Phi Delta Kappan, 93,* 20–25.

STUDENTS' REACTIONS 11

Schutz, P. A., Davis, H. A., & Schwanenflugel, P. J. (2002). Organization of concepts relevant to emotions and their regulation during test taking. *The Journal of Experimental Education, 70*(4), 316–342.

Sena, J. D. W., Lowe, P. A., & Lee, S. W. (2007). Significant predictors of test anxiety among students with and without learning disabilities. *Journal of Learning Disabilities, 40,* 370–376.

Spielberger, C. D., & Vagg, P. R. (Eds.). (1995). *Test anxiety: Theory, assessment and treatment.* Washington, DC: Taylor.

Swanson, S., & Howell, C. (1996). Test anxiety in adolescents with learning disabilities and behavior disorders. *Exceptional Children, 62,* 389–397.

Weiner, B. (1994). Integrating social and personal theories of achievement striving. *Review of Educational Research, 64,* 557–573.

Wigfield, A., & Eccles, J. S. (1989). Test anxiety in elementary and secondary school students. *Educational Psychologist, 24,* 159–183.

Zeidner, M. (1995a). Adaptive coping with test situations: A review of the literature. *Educational Psychologist, 30,* 123–133.

Zeidner, M. (1995b). Coping with examination stress: Resources, strategies, outcomes. *Anxiety, Stress, and Coping, 8,* 279–298.

Zeidner, M. (2007). Test anxiety in educational contexts: Concepts, findings, and future directions. In P. A. Schutz & R. Pekrun (Eds.), *Emotion in education* (pp. 165–184). In *Educational Psychology Series.* Burlington, MA: Academic Press.

First lines at the normal margin; subsequent lines indented (62)

Names repeated in subsequent entries (66)

Sequential page numbers (30)

Numbered table on a separate page (30)

Table title in italics (30)

Ruled lines to separate elements (30)

Column spacing adjusted for easy reading (31).

STUDENTS' REACTIONS 12

Table 1
Overall Responses (Security to Insecurity) to Question Types

	Rating					
Question type	1	2	3	4	5	6
Matching	25.8	30.3	23.6	11.2	3.4	5.6
True/false	31.4	25.8	24.7	13.5	3.4	1.1
Fill-in-the-blank	2.2	10.1	22.5	13.5	27.0	24.6
Multiple-choice	25.8	32.6	25.9	6.7	6.7	2.2
Listing	4.5	5.6	24.7	21.4	22.5	21.4
Essay	6.8	13.5	7.9	10.1	12.4	49.4

STUDENTS' REACTIONS 13

Numbered figure on a separate page (31–32)

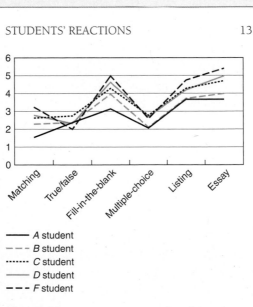

— *A* student
– – – *B* student
······· *C* student
—— *D* student
– – *F* student

Figure 1. Mean responses to questions by student grade categories.

STUDENTS' REACTIONS   14

Appendix

Test Anxiety Questionnaire

Survey: Test Anxiety—Reactions to Kinds of
Test Questions

M   F

Grade Last 9 Weeks: A   B   C   D   F

Circle one response for each kind of test question:
1 means that you feel *comfortable/secure* with these
kinds of questions (you won't worry about that part
of the test); *6* means that you feel *uncomfortable/
insecure* with these question types (you will worry
about how you do on that part of the test).
Consider tests for all classes, not just English.

	Secure		No reaction		Insecure
1. Matching	1	2	3	4	5	6
2. True/false	1	2	3	4	5	6
3. Fill-in-the-blank	1	2	3	4	5	6
4. Multiple-choice	1	2	3	4	5	6
5. Listing	1	2	3	4	5	6
6. Essay	1	2	3	4	5	6

Preparing PowerPoint and Poster Presentations

Presentations, essentially speeches supported by visual materials, provide unique opportunities. They allow you to share the results of either text-based or experimental research in visually oriented and interactive ways. Whether these presentations use a PowerPoint or poster format, the experience of preparing information in alternative ways develops helpful academic skills. In addition, presentations give you the chance to strengthen your ability to speak informatively to a group—an important professional skill.

A1 Preparing a PowerPoint Presentation

Originally designed for business applications, PowerPoint allows writers to prepare slides to illustrate ideas for presentations. In an academic setting, PowerPoint presentations allow students to share ideas and information in visually interesting ways.

Thinking About a Powerpoint Presentation

With its capability to include a wide range of graphic images, PowerPoint software allows you to create visual support for presentations. However, as you think about preparing and delivering a PowerPoint presentation, it is essential to remember that you and your ideas and information should be the primary focus, not the images on the slides.

Planning for a Powerpoint Presentation

In some instances, your presentation may be based on work for another class project; for example, the PowerPoint may be a class presentation of your research findings from a paper or report. In that case, the preliminary work is complete, and you can concentrate on the structure, design, and delivery elements of the presentation. In other instances, the presentation may be a fully separate project. In that case, research to secure your content and then turn your attention to structure, design, and delivery. In either circumstance, allow yourself sufficient time to complete the preliminary work, to prepare your slides, and to practice the presentation itself.

Thinking About Content—General Considerations

To get an overall sense of how to prepare PowerPoint slides most effectively, think about your content in a holistic way. Consider these suggestions.

- **Think about your time allotment.** Consider the level of detail you can include based on your time limit. A 5-minute presentation can provide only the broadest overview, whereas a 15-minute presentation can include more detail.

- **Consider your audience's level of knowledge.** What is your audience likely to know about the topic of your presentation? Will you need to define terms? Will you need to explain research methodology? Or is your audience conversant with the topic, terminology, and methods? The more your audience knows, the more directly you can approach your presentation.

- **Think about organization and development.** All presentations need a beginning, middle, and end, but the best presentations follow clear, familiar organizational patterns for the middle section: chronological order (historical overviews, descriptions of processes), order of importance (explanations of subtopics, persuasive arguments), comparison–contrast (reviews of alternative ideas, explanations of opposing views), and others. Arrange the topics of your presentation judiciously and then provide information and images that develop each topic.

NOTE: If your presentation is based on a paper or report, you can follow that structure *or* develop an alternative plan.

Thinking About Content—Specific Considerations

Once you have a general sense of how to focus your presentation, think about what specific content elements are needed for an effective presentation. Consider these recommendations.

- **Include a title slide.** Begin with a slide that includes the title of the presentation, your name, the course number and name, and the date. This slide functions like the title page of a paper or book and provides basic identifying information.

- **Consider including a preview slide.** As an option, include a slide that previews the main ideas of the presentation. Like a brief table of contents or a chapter preview, it lets your audience know the key points that you will address.

- **Present your information in a series of slides.** Prepare a series of slides that identify the main points, provide explanations and samples, and incorporate images. It is easier to follow a presentation with a large number of slides (when each contains a small amount of information) than it is to follow a presentation with only a few slides that contain too much information. (See "Thinking About Graphic Design" below.)

- **Consider using a summary slide.** As an option, include a slide at the end of your presentation that reiterates its main points. A simple presentation probably doesn't need a summary slide, but a longer one probably does.

- **Include a reference-list slide.** To acknowledge your sources, include a slide that contains citations for the materials you have used; it functions like the reference page of a paper. Make sure that the information is complete and that it is appropriately formatted.

- **Prepare a speaking script.** Develop an outline of key points from which to speak. Include references to your slides so that you remember to change slides at the appropriate time. Do not merely read from the slides; rather, provide a separate commentary that includes more information than the slides themselves contain. Also, include transitions between sections of the presentation to emphasize the logical connections between the elements.

NOTE: Many people find it helpful to transfer the speaking script onto numbered note cards (1-by-6 or 5-by-7 inches) because cards are easier to handle than sheets of paper.

- **Consider preparing a handout.** To provide a clear and helpful record of your presentation, prepare a one- to two-page handout that summarizes the ideas of the presentation. A handout prepared in prose allows you to articulate ideas fully and include many of the details from your speaking script, as well as the slides.

NOTE: If you give audience members only the printed slides, then you have given them only the visual portion of your presentation, omitting your important commentary.

Thinking About Graphic Design

The design of the slides themselves is a key element of a PowerPoint presentation. You should create slides that are appropriate to your topic and consistent with your approach. Consider these strategies.

- **Let the content guide you.** *What* you choose to put on a slide should determine *how* you present the slide. To present a three-step sequence, use a numbered list. To present four alternatives, use a bulleted list (which does not imply a specific order). To compare data, use a simple table. In other words, let the content and purpose guide the design, not the other way around.

- **Strive for visual clarity.** Because your audience will be listening to you, as well as looking at your slides, do not overload slides with unnecessary information or graphics.

- **Make basic design choices that suit your content.** PowerPoint provides a number of slide templates: a band of color at the top, a band of color down the side, an ink-splatter, a row of colored cubes, and so on. Use these familiar styles with the understanding that people may have seen them before. Alternatively, you can go online to secure additional template styles or create a unique style yourself. Whichever pattern you choose, avoid visual clutter and suit the style to the content.

NOTE: Create balance with your slides. Leave visual space at the margins and between elements (known as "white space" on typed documents) and make sure that all of the slides contain approximately the same amount of information or graphics.

- **Choose color themes carefully.** Because colors create impressions and indicate mood, select color palettes that complement, rather than detract from, your presentation. Vibrant colors (vivid pink, sunny yellow, bright blue, acid green) work best for informal or lighthearted topics, whereas subdued colors (maroon, gold, navy blue, avocado) work best for formal or serious topics. Colors used in small amounts (sidebars, ruled lines, frames) can be bold without being overwhelming. However, when colors are used generously (background, print), intense colors can become oppressive.

NOTE: If you choose color (rather than the standard black) for print features, make sure that it contrasts sufficiently with the background and can be easily read when projected.

- **Select fonts with care.** Choose font styles that are visually distinct when projected. Use large point sizes (24–36 is a reasonable range), so that audience members can read the text without difficulty. If you choose to vary fonts in your slides (for example, one font for titles and headings and a different font for primary text) or to vary point sizes (for example, 36 point for headings and 28 point for primary text), be sure to do so consistently.

NOTE: Avoid unusual decorative or display fonts. They project badly on some screens and can create an unprofessional impression.

- **Find images that enhance the presentation.** Include distinct visual elements that contribute to your presentation. Find images that are unique, make sure that they are of high quality, and reproduce their aspect ratio correctly. When possible, crop (cut down) the images to eliminate extraneous detail.

NOTE: Avoid familiar clip art images. Such works add nothing individual to your presentation. Instead, they are merely visual clichés, which can detract from your work.

- **Use charts, graphs, and tables when appropriate.** Use pie charts to show percentages, bar graphs to show comparisons, line graphs to show changes, and tables to show comparisons. Keep the designs simple and uncluttered, make the labels clear, and use color selectively for contrast.

- **Use numbered lists for sequential information.** When describing a process or a topic that must be addressed in a fixed order, use a numbered list. As with bulleted lists, use a small number per slide and make sure that the elements are presented in parallel form.

- **Use bullet points to present alternatives.** Because bullet points signal elements that are nonsequential and roughly equivalent, they are especially helpful in a PowerPoint presentation. Use a small number on each slide (generally 3–6), and make sure that the elements are presented in parallel form: words, phrases, or brief sentences.

- **Use audio selectively.** Because audio is often difficult to adjust for the space, use it selectively and always do a sound check before your presentation. Music can sometimes underscore a presentation, like the soundtrack of a film, and a spoken audio, if aptly chosen, can create interest. But sound effects (unless they are subtly used) are often disruptive or even comical—neither of which enhances your presentation.

- **Incorporate video clips when they serve a specific purpose.** Incorporating video links within a PowerPoint presentation can create a dynamic change of pace. However, the video clip must be well-selected, brief, and directly related to the content of your presentation. Before the presentation, test the clip using the equipment to ensure that the Web-link works.

- **Avoid visual clutter.** Keep the elements of each slide as uncluttered as possible. A few lines of text and some graphic elements are usually enough. While some people offer rigid guidelines (for example, no more than six lines and no more than six words per line), there are no "rules." However, the general principle of showing only a few elements at a time makes a great deal of sense.

- **Avoid "technical clutter."** PowerPoint provides a number of "animation" features: "cuts," "drop-in" elements, "fades," "reveals," "zooms," and others. While each feature can be interesting and purposeful, using too many suggests that technology, rather than content, is the focus of a presentation. Consequently, use animation features only if they serve content-related purposes. Otherwise, your audience will notice the technical "tricks," rather than the entire presentation.

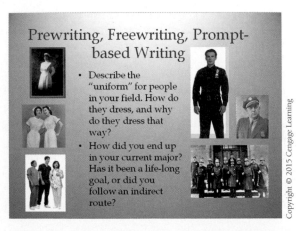

Effective PowerPoint slide

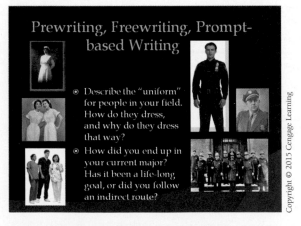

Ineffective PowerPoint slide

Thinking About Technical Matters

Because PowerPoint slides provide a limited amount of information and selected visual images, they need to be carefully done. An error that might go unnoticed on a double-spaced page of text stands out dramatically in the spare (and enlarged) image projected on a screen. Give special attention to these procedures.

- **Proofread for errors.** Review your slides to ensure that you have consistently capitalized words in bulleted lists, punctuated parallel elements in parallel ways, and double-checked mechanical elements (spelling, italics, line spacing, and so on).

- **Proofread your citations.** If a reference list is required, include complete information in correctly formatted citations.

Thinking About the Presentation

Because your comments will create the context for the PowerPoint slides, give serious attention to the "performance" elements of the presentation. Consider these strategies.

- **Analyze the room.** Think strategically about the presentation space. If the room is very large, modify the size of your images and adjust your speaking volume; if the room has windows without darkening shades, give special consideration to the clarity of your images; if the projection screen is small, then limit the amount of information on each slide. Also, think about your sight lines so that audience members can see both you and your slides.

- **Think about the equipment.** The size of the screen and the quality of the projection equipment will affect how you design your presentation. The larger the screen and the better the equipment, the more flexibility you will have. Because a wireless mouse allows you to control the projector from any location, use one if it is available.

NOTE: Do not assume, as many people do, that you can access your PowerPoint slides through an Internet connection in the presentation space. While this usually is workable, connections aren't always available. To avoid potential delays, embarrassment, or other problems, always take your PowerPoint on a flash drive.

- **Consider what to wear.** You don't necessarily need to wear a suit or a dress, but select clothing that looks polished and that isn't distracting. How you look has a bearing on the professionalism of the presentation.

- **Rehearse your comments.** Practice using your speaking script. As you rehearse, you will discover effective phrasing and suitable ways to explain ideas; in addition, the practice will help you feel more secure about what you have to say and how to say it best. It will also allow you to adjust your comments to fit the time limit.

- **Think about your delivery.** When you make your presentation, face the audience as much as possible—not the projection screen. Make eye contact with audience members in all parts of the room. If space and technology allow, move around the front of the room; stepping away from a lectern or podium creates a more dynamic performance. Speak loudly enough that you can be heard throughout the room, pace yourself so that you don't seem rushed, and be enthusiastic. Most of all, don't stand at the podium and read the slides—without question, the dullest approach to a PowerPoint presentation.

- **Plan for questions.** Think critically and predict questions that your audience might pose; then practice responding to those questions.

- **Think about how to incorporate a handout.** If your presentation is substantive and you have prepared a handout, plan to distribute it *after* the presentation. Tell your audience in your introductory comments that you will share a handout after the presentation so that they won't spend time taking notes.

PowerPoint presentations provide a dynamic and visually oriented way to share the results of research. Their multidimensional approach—the blending of printed text, graphics, and oral presentation—makes them an effective means to share the results of your research work.

A2 Preparing a Poster Presentation

Poster presentations developed as part of professional meetings. Recognizing that traditional, speech-based sessions limited the scope of conferences, organizers searched for ways in which to involve a greater number of researchers in conference activities, as well as to provide opportunities for people to share preliminary findings or to solicit reactions to "work in progress." Because poster presentations are now a common way to share research, teachers have begun to incorporate the format into their classroom activities so that student researchers can develop skills in presenting their findings in interactive ways.

Thinking About a Poster Presentation

Poster presentations emphasize visual elements, supported with printed information, and allow researchers to discuss their work with interested people.

At conferences, presenters are allotted a predetermined amount of space (4-by-4 feet, 4-by-8 feet, or sometimes more) in an exhibit hall and display their posters for review for an allotted amount of time (1 hour or sometimes longer). Presenters stay with their posters, explain their work, answer questions, and solicit reactions. The visual presentation of research findings provides an exciting alternative to traditional speeches (which are often readings of papers), and the interactive format allows for more give-and-take among those who attend conferences.

In classes and seminars, poster presentations allow students to present their research to the entire class, as opposed to just the teacher, and to gather helpful reactions to their work.

Identifying the Features of a Poster Presentation

Whether given at a conference or in a classroom, poster presentations share a variety of features, which may be surprisingly simple or highly elaborate.

- **Display surface.** The simplest poster can be prepared on a standard 2-by-3-foot sheet of poster board, mounted for stability. Displayed on an easel for easy viewing, this kind of poster is most commonly presented in the classroom. More elaborate posters are prepared as freestanding displays, may include multiple display panels, and may be quite expensive to prepare. Such complex posters are more commonly presented at conferences.

- **Content.** To ensure that people focus properly on your work, create a clear and interesting title for the poster and provide your name and affiliation. Because posters of all kinds must present content in a concise, easily readable form, use headings judiciously. The standard divisions of a research paper—method, results, discussion, and others—provide familiar ways to divide the content of the poster, although other organizational patterns are also acceptable.

- **Visual elements.** Because posters emphasize the visual presentation of research findings, use graphic elements to your advantage. Arrange information for easy interpretation, remembering that readers scan visual documents in the same way they read: from left to right and from top to bottom. When possible, reduce material to bulleted lists for easy scanning. Select simple fonts in sizes that can be read from 3 to 6 feet away. Use tables, charts, graphs, and images to clarify ideas. Employ color, when possible, to create visual interest.

- **Supporting documents.** Provide a one- to two-page supporting document that summarizes the information presented on your poster. Label it clearly with the presentation's title and your identifying information; also include key elements from the poster. Make copies for those attending the conference or for class members.

- **Presentation.** You must facilitate the review of the poster. Without simply reading or summarizing the material for your audience (after all, they can do that), highlight key features and direct their attention to the most salient points. Also, be prepared to answer questions and guide discussion.

Planning for a Poster Presentation

Because poster presentations provide a unique opportunity to share research findings, a well-planned presentation takes time to prepare and requires unique kinds of effort. Consider these suggestions.

- **Allow yourself sufficient time.** Do not assume that a poster session is easy to prepare. Not only does it require initial research, but it also warrants specialized preparation that may be new to you if you are used to preparing only written documents. Also, because the presentation includes more kinds of elements—visual and speaking components, as well as written content—preparing the poster presentation should not be a rushed effort.

- **Experiment with design elements.** Explore alternative ways to design your poster. Prepare material in several formats (try different fonts and font sizes; use different color combinations; prepare tables *and* figures), and then decide which format creates the best visual effect.

- **Solicit reactions.** Seek responses to your work. Ask for overall reactions but also ask specific questions about presentational elements. If you have prepared alternative versions of your poster, ask which is most effective.

- **Practice your presentation.** Although a well-prepared poster should in some regards "speak for itself," consider the ways in which you can help an audience review your poster. Develop a set of "talking points," a brief list of comments to guide your explanations. When possible, practice your presentation to ensure that your expression is clear and helpful.

- **Anticipate questions.** Think critically and predict questions that your audience might pose; then practice responding to those questions.

Poster presentations provide a unique way to share the results of research. Their conciseness, visual clarity, and interactivity make them an effective means of sharing the results of your research work.

Students' Reactions to Kinds of Test Questions: A Piece of the Test-Anxiety Puzzle

Gabriel Stevenson
CIMT 451

Student Research Day
May 4, 2013

Student Programs
Hulman Memorial
Student Union

Participants

- 89 high school students
- 44 female students
- 45 male students
- enrolled in 9th-grade English class
- consolidated school in west-central Indiana

Materials: Brief Questionnaire

- identify gender
- English grade the previous 9 weeks
- 6-element questionnaire about question types (matching, true–false, fill-in-the-blank, multiple choice, listing, essay); 6-point Likert-type scale

Procedure:

- read the instructions aloud
- emphasize complete school experience
- allotted 10 minutes to complete the questionnaire
- most completed the questionnaire in fewer than 5 minutes

	SECURE		NO REACTION		INSECURE	
Question Type	**1**	**2**	**3**	**4**	**5**	**6**
Matching	25.8	30.3	23.6	11.2	3.4	5.6
True/false	31.4	25.8	24.7	13.5	3.4	1.1
Fill-in-the-blank	2.2	10.1	22.5	13.5	27.0	24.6
Multiple-choice	25.8	32.6	26.9	6.7	6.7	2.2
Listing	4.5	5.6	24.7	21.4	22.5	21.4
Essay	6.8	13.5	7.9	10.1	12.4	49.4

Sample Poster

Common Technical Problems

B1 Fragments
B2 Comma Splices and Fused Sentences
B3 Pronoun Reference
B4 Pronoun Case
B5 Positioning Modifiers
B6 Active and Passive Voice
B7 Possessives and Contractions
B8 Outlining

B1 Fragments

Fragments are capitalized and punctuated as if they were sentences, but instead, they are either subordinate clauses or phrases lacking subjects or verbs.

Although fragments are common in speech, notes, rough drafts, and writing that imitates speech, fragments should be used only for special emphasis in formal writing.

Without Subjects or Verbs

Correct a fragment that lacks a subject or verb by supplying the missing element or by combining the fragment with a complete sentence.

Lacking Subjects

A fragment without a subject may be a verb phrase (a freestanding predicate or complement); it may also be a verbal phrase (a phrase using a gerund, a participle, or an infinitive). Eliminate a fragment lacking a subject either by adding a subject or by joining the fragment to an appropriate sentence.

During the Civil War, Clara Barton organized nursing care in makeshift hospitals. ^She Also founded the Red Cross.

[A subject has been added.]

Clara Barton's ~~had~~ one overriding goal, ^was To provide medical care to soldiers in the field.

[The infinitive phrase is joined to the sentence.]

Lacking Verbs

A fragment without a verb is usually a subject and related modifiers, an appositive, or an absolute phrase. Correct a fragment lacking a verb by adding a verb or by joining the appositive or absolute phrase to another sentence.

Dragnet, a popular police drama during the 1950s, ^it developed a strong following during its eight years on NBC.

[The fragment has been joined to a related sentence.]

Subordinate Clauses

A subordinate clause must be joined to an independent clause to form a grammatical sentence. Correct a subordinate-clause fragment by dropping the subordinating conjunction to form a simple sentence or by joining the subordinate clause to an independent clause.

Many people with mental health problems do not seek help. Because the stigma is sometimes too great.

[The subordinate clause becomes part of a complex sentence.]

Special Uses of Fragments

A fragment can be effective and acceptable when it is used to isolate and thus emphasize a key word or phrase. Use this strategy selectively to achieve emphasis or to supply an answer to a question.

Olivia Benson, Temperance Brennan, Christine Cagney, Allison Dubois, Jessica Fletcher, Brenda Johnson, Mary Beth Lacey, and Jane Tennison. These female characters populate crime dramas and help to create the strong followings that their shows garner. Do they resemble the real detectives who work in the real world? Of course not. But viewers look to crime dramas for entertainment, not for documentary accuracy.

B2 Comma Splices and Fused Sentences

Comma splices and fused sentences contain two or more independent clauses that are not properly punctuated. In a comma splice (also called a comma fault), the independent clauses are incorrectly joined with only a comma. In a fused sentence (also called a run-on sentence), independent clauses are placed one after the other with no punctuation.

Correct comma splices and fused sentences by changing the punctuation or the structure of the sentence.

Forming Two Sentences

Correct a comma splice or a fused sentence by forming two sentences.

More elderly Americans than people realize suffer from early-onset Alzheimer's disease⊙they are often seen as merely forgetful.

Using a Semicolon

Correct a comma splice or a fused sentence by using a semicolon to separate the independent clauses.

Most industrialized countries have national health care; the United States is a notable exception.

Using Coordinating and Subordinating Conjunctions

Use a coordinating conjunction (*and, but, for, nor, or, so,* or *yet*) with a comma to link independent clauses to form a compound sentence. As an alternative, use a subordinating conjunction (*although, because, since, while,* or others) to join independent clauses to form complex or compound-complex sentences.

Comma Splice

The Department of Homeland Security raised the security levels/ because
Internet "chatter" suggested that terrorist activity was possible.

[When the subordinate clause ends the sentence, a comma is unnecessary if the meaning is clear.]

Fused Sentence

Although
↗Police work is sometimes intense and stressful⌃ it is more frequently procedural and mundane.

[When the subordinate clause begins the sentence, a comma is
required.]

Conjunctive Adverbs

A conjunctive adverb (*besides, furthermore, however, nevertheless,
still, then, therefore*, and others) connects ideas logically but does
not link independent clauses grammatically. When a conjunctive
adverb appears in a comma splice or fused sentence, correct the
sentence by using a period or semicolon to separate the independent
clauses.

Teachers and administrators usually work well together⍮however,
their unique perspectives sometimes create tension.

[The use of a semicolon grammatically separates the two independent clauses.]

B3 Pronoun Reference

To create variety and unity in your writing, substitute pronouns for
overused nouns, following accepted patterns of pronoun usage.

Unclear Pronoun References

An unclear pronoun reference results when an antecedent is
ambiguously placed, broad or vague, or implied rather than
stated.

Ambiguous References

An ambiguous reference results when more than one noun could
be a pronoun's antecedent.

Ambiguous

Even though Patrick would only be working part time, the administrator gave him a detailed history of the prison facility. *He*
thought the lecture was a waste of time.
[Did the administrator feel dissatisfied, or did Patrick?]

Clear

Even though he thought the lecture was a waste of time, the administrator gave Patrick a detailed history of the prison facility.
[The rule of nearness suggests that *he* refers to the administrator.]

Vague References

A vague reference results when an antecedent is general or broad.

Vague

During the hearing, representatives of the Centers for Disease Control and Prevention presented information about the success of education programs and requested a larger budget. *This* was approved by Congress.
[Did Congress approve of the education programs' success, or did Congress approve the larger budget?]

Clear

Upon the request of representatives of the Centers for Disease Control and Prevention, Congress approved a larger budget.

Implied References

An implied antecedent suggests a reference but does so confusingly.

Unclear

The Booneville Educational Center is not efficiently organized, but *they* manage to deliver effective tutorials and workshops.
[*They* has no direct and clear antecedent.]

Clear

Although the director of the Booneville Educational Center is not efficiently organized, he manages to hire instructors who deliver effective tutorials and workshops.

Reflexive Pronouns and Subjects of Sentences

A reflexive pronoun serves only as an indirect or direct object.

While acknowledging the important work of first responders and ambulance staff, Dr. McDonald rightfully gave *herself* credit for establishing the ER procedures that probably saved the patients' lives.

Use a personal pronoun in place of a reflexive pronoun if the subject of the sentence is not the antecedent. A reflexive pronoun should never be the subject of a sentence.

Incorrect

Laura and *myself* disagree about the ethics of using the writing of incarcerated students in our scholarly work, whether attributed or not.

Correct

Laura and *I* disagree about the ethics of using the writing of incarcerated students in our scholarly work, whether attributed or not.

Clear Pronoun References

When a pronoun and its antecedent are separated by too many words, references become vague or unclear. Additionally, when too many pronouns are used sequentially, the writing becomes repetitive. To avoid potential confusion and to improve style, alternate between using a noun and using a pronoun. Such use also helps to establish clarity and to avoid monotony.

Jonas Salk, a researcher and virologist, is best known for the discovery of the polio vaccine. After *he* graduated from New York University School of Medicine, *he* (Salk) chose to research rather than to practice medicine. While at the University of Pittsburgh School of Medicine, *he* began work on a polio vaccine. *He* (Salk) assembled an exceptional research team, and *he* initiated the largest clinical trial in history—involving 1,800,000 children. Although *he* (Salk) was clearly proud of *his* important contribution, *he* always acknowledged the work of others, and *he* did not seek a patent for the polio vaccine. Rather, *he* (Salk) continued *his* professional work: *he* wrote four books, and *he* worked on an HIV vaccine during *his* last years.

[Although the entire paragraph is about Salk and consequently is not confusing, it is improved by alternating Salk's name with pronouns.]

For clarity, observe the convention of restricting pronoun references to sentences *within the same paragraph,* even when the reference seems clear.

The tradition of selflessness that~~,~~ _^he~~y~~ ^Salk^ represented so well is challenged today by researchers—and even research institutions—who thrive on publicity and strive to garner profits. . . .

B4 Pronoun Case

The case of a pronoun indicates the pronoun's grammatical relationship to the other words in the sentence. Pronoun case is indicated by changes in form (*I, me,* or *mine,* for example) or by changes in position in the sentence, as in the following example.

subj. case		obj. case	poss. case	
I	gave	them	his	address.

A pronoun used as a subject or as a predicate pronoun (a pronoun used in place of a predicate noun) is in the subjective case. A pronoun used as a direct object, indirect object, or object of a preposition is in the objective case. A noun or pronoun used to show ownership is in the possessive case.

Case Forms of Personal Pronouns

	SUBJECTIVE	OBJECTIVE	POSSESSIVE
Singular			
1st person	I	me	my, mine
2nd person	you	you	your, yours
3rd person	he, she, it	him, her, it	his, her, hers, its
Plural			
1st person	we	us	our, ours
2nd person	you	you	your, yours
3rd person	they	them	their, theirs

Case Forms of *Who* and Related Pronouns

SUBJECTIVE	OBJECTIVE	POSSESSIVE
who	whom	whose
whoever	whomever	

Usually a pronoun changes form to produce the possessive case (*I, my; she, her*); however, an indefinite pronoun (*someone, everybody*) forms the possessive by adding *'s* (*someone's, everybody's*).

A possessive-case pronoun, which does not use an apostrophe, should not be confused with a contraction that sounds the same: *its* and *it's* ("it is"), *theirs* and *there's* ("there is"), and *whose* and *who's* ("who is").

Subjective Case

A pronoun used as the subject of a sentence or clause is in the subjective case.

Subjective Case

Although *she* began her career as a lawyer, Janet Napolitano's work as a judge, attorney general, and governor prepared her well for her role as Secretary of the Department of Homeland Security.

When a sentence has a compound subject, isolate the parts of the subject to help you choose the appropriate pronoun.

Compound Subject

Warren Burger and William Rehnquist were the longest-serving Chief Justices of the Supreme Court. Burger and *he* served six years longer than other justices in the 20th century.
[Burger served; *he* served; consequently, *Burger and he served.*]

Because a predicate pronoun restates the subject, it requires the subjective case. If this construction sounds too formal, invert the subject and the predicate pronoun.

During triage, we learned that the chief organizer was *he*.
[The predicate pronoun, signaled by the linking verb *was*, must be in the subjective case.]

During triage, we learned that *he* was the chief organizer.
[This sentence sounds less formal.]

Objective Case

A pronoun used as a direct object or as an indirect object must be in the objective case.

Direct Object

In developing the fourth amendment to the U.S. Constitution, the founders established protections against unreasonable searches and seizures; we should honor *them* for that.

Indirect Object

Although judges who deny search warrants may seem to protect suspected criminals, we should give *them* credit for protecting individual rights.

Object of Preposition

People from all walks of life surely realize that the fourth amendment establishes essential protections for *them*.

When a preposition has a compound object, isolate the parts of the object to help you select the appropriate pronoun

After the terrorist attacks on September 11, 2001, President Bush and Attorney General Ashcroft pushed for legislation that to some degree compromises the fourth amendment. Although many law makers were involved, most of the attention was directed at *him* and Ashcroft.
[at *him*; at Ashcroft]

Possessive Case

Possessive Pronouns Used With Nouns

A possessive pronoun—*my, your, his, her, its, our, your*, or *their*—modifies a noun. It acts as an adjective and is sometimes called a pronoun-adjective.

Tamika and Marcus received the same grades in classes and the same evaluations for clinicals. However, *her* scores on the Board exam were slightly better than *his* results.
[The pronouns in the possessive case serve as pronoun-adjectives.]

Possessive Pronouns Used Alone

The possessive pronouns *mine, yours, his, hers, its, ours, yours*, or *theirs* are sometimes used alone. Each can act as a subject, predicate pronoun, direct object, or object of a preposition.

Given the size of the crowd and the physical irregularity of the location, the responsibility for the lack of perimeter control was only partly *theirs*.

Possessive Pronouns Modifying a Gerund

When modifying a gerund (an *-ing* verb that functions as a noun), a pronoun must be in the possessive case, serving as a pronoun-adjective.

I was annoyed by *his* snickering during the parent-teacher conference.
[The annoyance resulted from the person's *snickering*, not from the person himself.]

The supervisor commented that *their* handling of paperwork was both timely and meticulous.
[The best part was their *handling of paperwork*, not them.]

Appositives and Elliptical Constructions

Pronouns in Appositives

When a pronoun is part of an appositive that restates the subject of a clause, the pronoun is in the subjective case. When it restates an object, the pronoun is in the objective case.

The two precinct captains, *she* and Gerald, were responsible for preparing the weekly reports.
[Because the phrase *she and Gerald* restates the subject of the sentence (*two precinct captains*), the pronoun must be in the subjective case.]

The chief of police sent a memo stating that recommendations for procedural changes be sent to the precinct captains, Gerald and *her*.
[*Gerald and her* restates *precinct captains*, the object of the preposition *to*; therefore, the pronoun must be in the objective case.]

We or Us With Nouns

When using *we* or *us* with a noun, choose the case that would be correct if the noun were omitted.

The cliché is true: *We* Americans take many of our freedoms for granted.
    [Without *Americans*, the pronoun appears correctly in the subjective case.]

Pronouns in Elliptical Constructions

An elliptical construction (a construction in which words are omitted or understood) uses the case that would be appropriate if all the words were included. If the pronoun used alone sounds too formal, add the omitted words.

The clinic's stress counselor arrived twenty minutes later than *we*.
    [It is understood that the counselor arrived twenty minutes later than *we arrived*.]

Who and *Whoever* and *Whom* and *Whomever*

Who and *Whoever*

Use the subjective case form—*who* or *whoever*—as the subject of a sentence, clause, or question.

Jack Kevorkian, a pathologist *who* supported physician-assisted suicide, was commonly known in the media as "Dr. Death."
    [*Who* is the subject of the clause.]

Like most confrontational activists, Kevorkian would make frank and often startling observations to *whoever* would listen—reporters, interviewers, or commentators.
    [*Whoever* is the subject of the clause; although the preposition *to* might suggest that the objective case is required, the whole clause, not the word *whoever*, is the object of the preposition.]

Whom and *Whomever*

Use the objective-case form—*whom* or *whomever*—as a direct object, indirect object, or object of a preposition.

Whom should we propose for the vacant seat on the advisory board of the Community Safety Council?
    [*Whom* is the direct object of *propose*.]

The board will probably appoint *whomever* we select.
    [*Whomever* is the direct object of *select*.]

B5 Positioning Modifiers

Position modifiers—which explain, describe, define, or limit a word or group of words—so that the relationship between them and the words they modify is clear.

Clarity and Smoothness

Place modifiers where they create clear meaning.

Long Modifiers

If a long modifier separates the subject from the verb or the verb from the object, reposition the modifier.

Jeffrey Toobin's *The Nine: Inside the Secret World of the Supreme Court,* a behind-closed-doors account of the workings of the nation's highest court, is both fascinating and informative.

Prepositional Phrases

Because nearness guides modification, place prepositional phrases near the words they modify.

Because of her controversial positions on drug use and contraception, Dr. Mildred Jefferson criticized Dr. Joycelyn Elders's work as Surgeon General.

[Elders, not Jefferson, held the controversial views.]

Limiting Modifiers

Place limiting modifiers such as *hardly*, *nearly*, or *only* with care and double-check to see that the meaning of the sentence is clear.

He simply stated the problem.
[Stating the problem is all he did.]

He stated the problem simply.
[He made the problem easy to understand.]

Modifiers Near Infinitives

Under most circumstances, do not position a modifier between the elements of an infinitive: *to* and a verb. Although this usage is common in speech and some kinds of writing, it is best to avoid split infinitives.

After rereading his notes, Dr. Martinez began to quickly prepare his report.

Dangling Modifiers

When a phrase at the beginning of a sentence does not modify the subject of the sentence, it is a dangling modifier. Reposition the misplaced phrase.

Alternately celebratory or outraged, the courtroom erupted with reactions from the people present.

[The people, not the courtroom, had strong reactions.]

Squinting Modifiers

A squinting modifier is a word or phrase that could modify either the words before it or the words after it. Reposition the element to avoid confusion or use the relative pronoun *that* to clarify your meaning.

The mediator said before ten o'clock they could conclude the proceedings.

[This repositioning clarifies a ten o'clock conclusion of the proceedings; alternately, moving the phrase *before ten o'clock* to the beginning of the sentence would emphasize the time at which the mediator spoke.]

B6 Active and Passive Voice

Active and passive voice establishes the significance of main ideas and helps to create focus in writing. Consequently, the choices you make control your meaning.

Active and Passive Sentences

Active Sentences

In an active sentence, the subject of the sentence acts.

Transportation Security Administration officers now screen passengers using full-body scanners.

Passive Sentences

In a passive sentence, the subject of the sentence is acted upon. A passive verb requires auxiliaries. While a passive sentence does not always specify the person completing the action, when it does, the person is named in a prepositional phrase beginning with *by*.

Passengers are now screened by Transportation Security Administration officers using full-body scanners.

Emphasis: Who or What Acts

An active sentence emphasizes the doer of an action. It establishes a clear, strong relationship between the subject and verb.

The patient's lifestyle clearly compromised her general health.
[The patient's compromised health is clearly due to her choices.]

When the results of an action are more important than the doer of the action or when the doer is unknown, passive sentences effectively express the meaning.

The patient's health was further compromised by a misdirected care plan.

Using an active or a passive verb allows subtle but significant shifts in meaning and emphasis.

Active

In 2007, criminals stole an estimated $16 billion in property in the United States.
[The use of *criminals* with the active verb *stole* emphasizes the actions of criminals.]

Passive

An estimated $16 billion in property was stolen in the United States in 2007.
[This sentence shifts the emphasis to the value of the stolen property.]

Emphasis: Repeated Action

The passive voice emphasizes the action over the doer of the action; thus, it is especially useful for describing universal or widespread conditions or events.

Passive

Having a colonoscopy is now a common procedure for people over 50.
[The procedure is most important here, not the individual doctors who perform it.]

Active

Doctors commonly perform colonoscopies on people over 50.
[This construction emphasizes the doctors who perform the procedures.]

Generally, write active sentences when "who is doing what" is most important. When "what is being done" is most important, passive sentences serve your purpose better.

B7 Possessives and Contractions

Use apostrophes to show possession (usually with an added *s*) and to indicate the omission of letters or numbers from words or dates.

Possessive Case

Singular Nouns

Form the possessive of a singular noun (either common or proper) by adding 's

COMMON NOUNS	PROPER NOUNS
operating room's features	Atticus's closing arguments
boss's recommendations	J. Edgar Hoover's legacy
building's perimeter	New Orleans's hospitals

Plural Nouns

Form the possessive of a plural noun ending in *s* (either common or proper) by adding an apostrophe only; an additional *s* is unnecessary. Form the possessive of an irregular plural noun that does not end in *s* (*children*, for example) by adding 's.

teachers' lounge   the Madoffs' legal counsel
But:
children's advocates   women's rights

To check whether a possessive form is correct, eliminate the 's or just the apostrophe. The word remaining should be the correct one for your meaning. For example, the phrase *student's complaints* refers to only one student; the phrase *students' complaints* refers to multiple students.

Compound Words and Joint Possession

Form the possessive of a compound word or indicate joint possession in a series by adding 's to the last noun only.

brother-in-law's surgery

New York, Los Angeles, and Chicago's combined crime statistics

If possession in a series is not joint but individual, each noun in the series must be possessive.

Meirhold's, Vandes's, and Chaney's fingerprints
[Each person has a separate set of fingerprints.]

Omission of Letters and Numbers

Use an apostrophe to form a contraction and to create an abbreviated version of a date, with some of the numbers omitted. Contractions and abbreviated dates are best used in informal writing. In formal writing, present names and dates fully.

WITH APOSTROPHE	COMPLETE FORM
shouldn't	should not
I'll	I will or I shall
the '98 report	the 1998 report

Not With Possessive Pronouns

Do not use an apostrophe with a possessive pronoun. Do not be confused by those that end in –s (*yours, ours, his,* and others).

The child's parents completed the family-history questionnaire; the information was *theirs*.
[not *their's*].

The medical technician asked for clarifications and entered the information into the database; the responsibility for the completed work was hers.
[not *her's*].

[Apostrophes in *their's* and *her's* would indicate contracted forms—*their is* and *her is*—which are nonsensical. Clearly, the possessive pronouns are correct.]

B8 Outlining

An outline is a structural plan using headings and subdivisions to clarify the main features of the paper and the interrelationships among them. Loosely structured, informal outlines provide simplicity and freedom, while highly systematic, formal outlines emphasize clarity and completeness.

In the earliest stages of drafting—when you are deciding what should come first, second, third, and so on—an informal outline works well. At later stages of writing—when you need to analyze your work for consistency, completeness, and logic—a formal outline is helpful. Importantly, informal and formal outlines are plans, not descriptions of what you *must* do. If your plan does not work, decide why and make the necessary changes.

An Informal Outline

An informal outline is intended for your use only. Consequently, it may follow a pattern that is uniquely yours, as long as it is consistent. Consider creating lists marked with numbers, arrows, dots, dashes, or any other convenient symbol to indicate relative importance among ideas.

This is a brief, informal outline for a paper on two important pieces of medical equipment.

Stethoscope (1816)

- René Laënnec
- Description
- Improvements
  - Golding Bird
  - Arthur Leared
  - George Cammann

Blood Pressure Meter (1881)

- Samuel Siegfried Karl Ritter von Basch
- Description
- Improvements
  - Scipione Riva-Rocci
  - Harvey Cushing

This is an informal outline for a paper on four particular murder trials.

Harry Thaw (1906)
- Thaw
- White
- Newspaper coverage

Leopold and Loeb (1924)
- Leopold and Loeb
- Bobby Franks
- Newspaper and radio coverage

Bruno Hauptmann (1935)
- Hauptmann
- The Lindbergh baby
- Newspaper and radio coverage

O. J. Simpson (1995)
- Simpson
- Nicole Brown and Ron Goldman
- Newspaper, radio, television, and Internet coverage

A Formal Outline

A formal outline is intended for readers. For this reason, it must adhere to the following conventions.

- Indicate major topics with uppercase Roman numerals (I, II, III).
- Indicate subdivisions of topics with uppercase letters (A, B, C).
- Indicate clarifications of subdivisions (examples, supporting facts, and so on) with Arabic numerals (1, 2, 3).
- Indicate details with lowercase letters (a, b, c).

In addition, a formal outline must adhere to the following structural conventions.

- **Use parallel forms throughout.** Use phrases and words in a topic outline and full sentences in a sentence outline. An outline may use full sentences for major topics and phrases in subdivisions of topics (a mixed outline) but should do so consistently.

- **Include only one idea in each entry.** Subdivide entries that contain more than one idea.

- **Include at least two entries at each sublevel.** If the topic can't be subdivided, then simply use the main element.

- **Indicate the inclusion of introductions and conclusions but do not outline their content.** Although they are important to the overall effect of the paper, introductions and conclusions are identified but not described. If you wish to include a thesis statement or research question, identify it clearly after the label for the introduction and before the formal outline begins.

- **Align headings of the same level at the same margin.**
When reviewing a formal outline, readers expect to find similar material presented in a similar way. Use consistent indentation patterns in the formal outline to show this degree of emphasis.

The formal outline presented next is a developed version of the informal outline on medical equipment that is included on pages 162–163.

INTRODUCTION

Thesis Statement: The invention of two pieces of medical equipment revolutionized the ways in which patients are examined.

I. Stethoscope (1816)
   A. René Laënnec
      1. French physician
      2. Necker-Enfants Malades Hospital
   B. Description
      1. Wooden tube
      2. Flanges at both ends
      3. Monaural (one ear)
      4. Resembled an "ear trumpet"
   C. Improvements
      1. Golding Bird (1840)
         a. Flexible tubing
         b. Still monoaural
      2. Arthur Leared (1851)
         a. Biaural (two ear)
         b. Improved earpieces
      3. George Cammann (1852)
         a. Refined design
         b. For commercial production
II. Blood Pressure Meter (1881)
   A. Samuel Siegfried Karl Ritter von Basch
      1. Austrian physician
      2. University of Vienna

  B. Description
    1. A cuff
    2. Measuring unit/gauge
    3. Inflation bulb and valve
  C. Improvements
    1. Scipione Riva-Rocci (1896)
      a. Improved design
      b. Easier use
    2. Harvey Cushing (1901)
      a. Refined design
      b. Promoted it commercially

CONCLUSION

The following formal outline is a developed version of the informal outline on murder trials that is included on page 163.

INTRODUCTION

Thesis Statement: America's fascination with wealth and privilege has often led to an inordinate interest in murder trials that involved people with money.

  I. Harry Kendal Thaw (1906)
    A. Thaw (defendant)
      1. Son of a wealthy industrialist
      2. History of mental problems
      3. Married to an actress who knew White
    B. Stanford White (victim)
      1. Partner in McKim, Mead, and White—a prestigious architectural firm
      2. Known for his lavish lifestyle
      3. Known for womanizing
    C. Sensational newspaper stories
  II. Nathan Leopold, Jr., and Richard Loeb (1924)
    A. Leopold and Loeb (murderers)
      1. Sons of wealthy businessmen
      2. Students at University of Michigan and University of Chicago
      3. Lovers

    B. Bobby Franks (victim)

        1. Son of Chicago millionaire

        2. Kidnapped

        3. Possibly tortured

        4. Killed

    C. Sensational newspaper and radio stories

III. Bruno Hauptmann (1935)

    A. Hauptmann (alleged murderer)

        1. German immigrant

        2. Some circumstantial evidence

    B. Child of Charles Lindbergh (victim)

        1. Son of the famous aviator

        2. Kidnapped from his bedroom

        3. Murdered

    C. Sensational newspaper and radio stories

IV. O. J. Simpson (1995)

    A. Simpson (alleged murderer)

        1. Famous football player

        2. Celebrity status

    B. Nicole Brown and Ronald Goldman (victims)

        1. Simpson's ex-wife

        2. Brown's current boyfriend

        3. Killed outside her condominium

    C. Sensational newspaper, radio, television, and Internet coverage

CONCLUSION

Index

Format for APA Reference-List Entries

1. Begin the first line at the left margin and indent subsequent lines ½ inch.
2. Invert the author's name so that the last name appears first; use first and middle initials.
3. When no author is named, list the source by title.
4. Place the publication date in parentheses, followed by a period.
5. Cite the complete title, including subtitles.
6. Use a period, followed by one space, to separate author, date, title, and publication information.

See Chapters 4 to 8 for additional information and examples.

Sample Reference-List Entries

An Article in a Journal With Continuous Paging (5a)

Harrison, R. L., & Westwood, M. J. (2009). Preventing vicarious traumatization of mental health therapists: Identifying protective practices. *Psychotherapy: Theory, Research, Practice, Training, 46,* 203–219.

An Article in a Journal With Separate Paging (5b)

McDonald, T. P., Poertner, J., & Jennings, M. A. (2007). Permanency for children in foster care: A competing risks analysis. *The Journal of Social Science Research, 33*(4), 45–56.

An Article in a Monthly Magazine (5d)

Gorman, C. (2010, October). Closing the health gap. *Scientific American, 303*(4), 34–36.

An Article in a Newspaper (5f)

Pogrebin, R. (2010, April 22). A mother's loss, a daughter's story. *The New York Times,* pp. E1, E9.

A Book by One Author (6a)

Weiner, M. F. (2010). *Power, protest, and the public school: Jewish and African American struggles in New York City.* New Brunswick, NJ: Rutgers University Press.

A Book by Two or More Authors (6b)

Wright, J. P., Tibbetts, S. G., & Daigle, L. E. (2008). *Criminals in the making: Criminality across the life course.* Thousand Oaks, CA: Sage.